Milestones in Irish History

Edited by

LIAM DE PAOR

A Companion Series to
The Thomas Davis Lectures

Published in collaboration with
Radio Telefís Éireann
by
THE MERCIER PRESS
CORK and DUBLIN

The Mercier Press Limited
4 Bridge Street, Cork
24 Lower Abbey Street, Dublin 1

British Library Cataloguing in Publication Data

Milestones in Irish history. —
1. Ireland — History
I. De Paor, Liam II. Radio Telefis
Eireann III. Series
941.5   DA910

ISBN 0 - 85342 - 762 - 3

Printed by Litho Press Co., Midleton, Co. Cork.

Contents

Preface

The thirteen lectures here printed with minor modification were delivered on RTE radio in the summer of 1983 and repeated in 1985. The purpose of the series was to provide for the radio audience the thoughts of a number of Irish scholars, mostly historians, on selected problems or episodes of Irish history. In general, each contribution has for its focus a significant event or episode of the past. But the intention was not just to provide a narrative account of these events, but rather to use each of them as a starting point for a discussion of some of the questions that arise from historical research.

There was a considerable and favourable public response to the broadcasts, and it is felt that the lectures should now be made available in print. As the work of research continues, with more and more detailed investigation of the documents of the past, not only does additional information come to light all the time, but it becomes possible, or sometimes necessary to change emphasis, to make reassessments and to revise judgments. Very often such revisions are at the expense of a simplification, often an over-dramatisation, of the past, but sometimes they simply add depth and colour to our understanding of what happened.

The 'milestones' chosen for this series span the whole range of time from early prehistory to the present, opening with Professor Mitchell's enquiry into the social and historical meaning of the building of the remarkable cemetery of megalithic tombs centred on the great monuments of Knowth, Dowth and Newgrange, along the River Boyne. Newgrange is visited by many thousands of visitors every year, and a large proportion of them must come away with questions in their minds about the people who built it in the far distant past. To these questions Professor Mitchell addresses his talk.

My own contribution looks at the background of the work of a figure who is at one and the same time one of the best known, one of the least known and one of the most controversial in Irish history: St Patrick. Then: was Clontarf, in 1014, the great liberating battle which freed Ireland from the tyrannical rule of the Danes? This is how it used to be presented in a romantic view which, as Professor Ó Corráin shows, owes more to fiction than to history. Dr Richter examines another episode which we have all learned to look on as epochal: the advent of the Normans.

The later talks deal with modern times, beginning with the episode which is universally taken as marking the significant moment in the downfall of the Gaelic system of early and medieval Ireland: the departure from Irish shores of the Earls of Tyrone and Tyrconnell, studied by Dr Margaret Mac-Curtain. This is balanced, as it were, by an investigation of the new order that was created in place of the old, in Dr Clarke's look at the Plantations of Ulster: Two major political developments are examined by James McGuire, who considers the meaning and background of the Act of Union which made Ireland a part of the United Kingdom in 1801 and Professor Kevin B. Nowlan, who looks at the major achievement of Daniel O'Connell's earlier career, the further Act which gave Catholic Emancipation in 1829.

Processes involving large-scale cultural and social change are looked at by Dr R. B. Walsh, who traces the decline of the Irish language, by Professor McCartney who examines the great effort made to revive it at the turn of the century, and by Professor Lee, who analyses the long-drawn-out struggle over the possession of land. Two investigations of twentieth-century questions bring us right down to the preoccupations of the present. Dr Ronan Fanning gives his views on the partitioning of Ireland, which in formal and legal terms occurred in 1920, and Professor John A. Murphy concludes with a look at the historical meaning of Ireland's entry to the European Economic Community in 1973.

It will be plain that this collection does not constitute a continuous outline of Irish history from the beginning until now. Rather it provides a series of glimpses, illuminated by the thoughts of people whose vocation it is to investigate these matters. But the glimpses are spaced to form a continuity of kind, markers, or 'milestones' along a road.

Liam de Paor
Dublin 1986

1. The Builders of the Boyne Tombs

Frank Mitchell

The three great Egyptian pyramids at Giza have long been regarded as among the seven wonders of the world, but in their own way the three great tombs of the Boyne valley, Dowth, Newgrange, and Knowth, built at the same time as the pyramids, two thousand five hundred years before the birth of Christ, are just as amazing. The pyramids of Egypt were royal tombs, intended to hold no more than a few members of the ruling family; the Boyne tombs received the cremated remains of hundreds of people, not all of whom can have been of high social status, though they were probably related by kinship. Who were these people, and how did they both amass the wealth and gain the technical skill that were necessary for the erection of such mausolea?

Gordon Childe, a very distinguished archaeologist, used to speak of the Neolithic revolution which first made possible the amassing of wealth and the emergence of a capitalist economy. The miser and his hoard are proverbial, but some means of hoarding is essential if wealth is to be built up. The hoard may be of gold or diamonds, or more prosaically of grain or flesh. Today the storehouses of the EEC are overflowing with hoards of barley and meat, sold into intervention.

If you have no knowledge of growing grain or domesticating animals then you cannot build up a reserve of foodstuffs, and you must spend your life in an endless round of hunting and fishing and gathering roots, nuts and berries. You have neither the time nor the means for elaborate tomb-building.

But about eight thousand years ago, somewhere in the Middle East, in Syria or Mesopotamia, some men began to cultivate wild barleys and wheats and to domesticate the sheep and the cow. If carefully dried, the cereal grains can be stored for years, and a herd of cows stores meat just as effectively as a cold store. For cultivation the soil had to be broken, and for this purpose a stone mounted on a stick was necessary. Earlier men had used implements of chipped stone, but the farmers found that a polished edge was more efficient on mattocks for digging and axes for cutting. They also discovered the art of baking moulded clay into durable pottery for storing grain and other commodities. Because of these developments, farming, polishing stone and making pottery, their cultural status is styled Neolithic or New Stone Age, and these are the people of Childe's Revolution.

If you have a reserve of food, starvation becomes less common as a cause of death, and the population increases in number. This increase brings a greater demand for food. and new land must be brought into cultivation, herds must increase in number, if the necessary food is to be provided. There was no available land for younger sons, and so they radiated outwards carving out new farmsteads wherever suitable land could be found. Some drifted northwestwards into and across Europe, the boundaries of their farms advancing each year by perhaps half a mile, until the advance had to halt on the shores of the English Channel. Four thousand years had gone by since they had been forced out of the birthplace of farming in the Middle East.

Both in Britain and in Ireland there was already a population, though probably very small in number, of bands of food-gatherers who knew nothing of settled farming, but were constantly on the move. The march of the seasons would bring concentrated runs of salmon in the rivers, flocks of wintering ducks on the lakes, abundance of hazelnuts and blackberries in autumn, and the food-gatherers wandered like gypsies collecting every variety of food that the seasons offered. They had no settled bases, and no heartland which they would wish to defend from invaders. But like all men throughout the ages they were hungry for new ideas, for new technical advances.

One great problem constantly occupies all archaeologists – How do new ideas spread? How are technical advances propagated? In olden days invasion was regarded as the key. You had the new idea, you advanced into the territory of those who had not, and those who survived your advance absorbed your ideas. Other archaeologists say No invasion: for them diffusion is all. The English Channel and the Irish Sea do not offer insuperable barriers even to primitive people, and modest comings and goings would enable intelligent people to grasp the new concepts without these being bodily transported by invaders. An Irish aborigine who crossed into Britain would stand amazed at the carefully tended crops of growing grain and gape at the enormous animals which were shambling about in compounds, not being hunted but being carefully tended. If he became aware of what was going on he could perhaps steal a small supply of seed-corn, just as in the nineteenth century seeds of the rubber tree were smuggled out of Brazil to found the rubber plantations of the Far East, in Java and Sumatra.

But you cannot diffuse a cow across a stretch of open water. You must transport it in a boat. This is a difficult task, calling for imagination, skill and courage, and the people who carried it out were the ancestors of those who built the great tombs in the Boyne Valley, a feat which again required much imagination, and great skill and courage.

Suppose you are a young man hungry for land standing at Calais looking at the chalk cliffs of Dover, or standing in Scotland looking at the chalk cliffs at Larne, every fibre in you will urge you to cross the water by hook or by crook and seize new land for yourself and your family. What sort of Ireland do you see from Scotland? Stretching up the slopes of the Antrim plateau you will see a continuous sheet of oakwood. This does not either surprise or depress you as this is the sort of woodland you and your forbears have hacked your way through for many generations. At first the heavy canopy of the trees looks forbidding, but if you take off a ring of bark right round the trees, the trees will quickly die. Sunlight can now flood the soil which is rich in fertile leaf mould, and with the aid of your handled mattock armed with a blade of polished stone you can break up the soil and sow your grain among the dead trees. If there are fallen trees, or you want wood for a house or for fence-posts, you have also a polished stone axe for your carpentry work.

If you look at the shoreline below the cliffs you will see thin plumes of smoke arising from the fires of the aboriginal food-gatherers, grilling the fish and the lobsters they have taken, and gorging on the oysters and cockles they have easily collected on the shore. These fires do not disturb you, as you have met them before on lake-shores and river-banks in northern Britain. The makers of the fires were few in number and rather elusive; head-on clashes with them were rare, you sometimes bartered fish and fowl from them, and gradually they acquired your ways and became absorbed into your culture. It was to be the same in Ireland.

One thing you did have to have – a boat to transport your cows, your sheep and your pigs. The raw materials were to hand, wood to provide the frame, and hides from slaughtered cattle to provide a watertight skin, exactly the materials that were until recently used to build the curraghs of the Aran Islands, boats whose ancestry must go back for thousands of years. The modern curragh would have been too small for your purpose, you had to have a larger boat.

But how large? Where would you draw the line between size and manoeuvrability? If the cattle were to get ashore, the landing would have to be on an open beach. The boat would have to have a shallow draught, and yet be strong enough to bear some pounding by the waves. A calm day would be necessary for the crossing, and such days were rare. A large boat with some carrying capacity would reduce the number of trips to transport at least two bulls and two adult cows, the minimum necessary to build up a new herd. Men had also to be carried to unload the cargo, once safely across. A curragh-type boat, with a crew of nine, and a carrying capacity of about three tons would probably have been right.

You also had to know where you were heading for; and almost certainly preliminary forays were made. When in World War II it was decided to make a landing in Normandy the most elaborate investigations and rehearsals were made, even going to mock-landings at other places. And if the Allies in Normandy were venturing all, similarly the Neolithic farmers were venturing all. Weather, beaches, tides, currents, all had to be considered. Possibly even site-preparations had been made some seasons before the stock were to be moved. Groups of men could have made the crossing, prepared clearings in the woodlands, assembled fodder reserves of dried leaves and twigs, so that the amount of material to be transported by boat could be minimised.

A whole kinship group had to be moved, men, women, children and infants, together with breeding and milking livestock and corn. The timing was also important. It could not be before the end of August because the home crops had to be harvested for the last time, and had to be before the storms of winter would make the crossing still more perilous. Clearly courage as well as skill was called for.

And there must have been plenty of such groups on the move. The crossing of the English Channel took place about four thousand years before the birth of Christ, and once established the farmers quickly moved on, reaching even the Shetland Islands before another five hundred years had elapsed. Our first Irish record is about three thousand five hundred years before the birth of Christ.

In this outline account of the expansion of farming across Europe I have oversimplified, because differing groups followed different routes. One group followed a western route up along the Atlantic coast, from Spain and Portugal through Brittany, across Cornwall and the Scilly Isles, and on into Ireland. In such farming communities the idea of the kinship group was always very strong, and a group that was united in life would think of a continuation of that unity after death, and how could this be better exemplified than in a common tomb for the dead? On the rocky coasts of western Europe stone was abundant, and durable structures of large stones, often described as megalithic, began to be erected to serve as tombs. Such structures imply a belief in a life after death, an ability for appropriate design, and technical skill to carry out the design.

A tunnel was created by erecting two parallel lines of large stones and covering them by roofing-slabs at right angles. At the inner end of the tunnel or passage a slightly wider chamber was created in the same way. The structure was then buried by the heaping up of stones on top to create a mound or cairn. The edge of the mound was defined by an enclosing ring or kerb of elongated stones laid end to end. Today this type of tomb is commonly referred to as a Passage-grave. Important stones both in the tomb and in the encircling kerb were then decorated by cutting designs into them with the aid of stone chisels. On the whole the motifs were abstract, snake-like lines, zig-zags, lozenges, spirals, circles, but there are designs with paired circles close together like eyes, and other curves which can be read as stylised representations of the human form. Cremation was the standard practice, and the burned bones were then deposited in the tomb. In cases in recent years when the contents of the tombs have been carefully excavated no weapons have been found, but only occasional beads and fragments of a characteristic type of pottery.

It is presumptuous even to guess at the type of burial ceremony that took place and thus at a further remove at the beliefs implied, but it is clear that they differed from those of some other primitive peoples who held that the next world will be much the same as this one, a place of battle and strife. Those who held this view, like the pagan Vikings, were buried with full fighting equipment, sword, shield, spear and battle-axe. We may picture the body prepared for cremation, still adorned with personal jewellery, perhaps in a shroud, with a pottery vessel containing food for the last journey by its side. The ashes would then be carried into the tomb. Still more daringly we can see the dark passage and the chamber as a womb in which the remains will rest until the time comes for them to be born again.

Progressive Neolithic farmers, whose religious expression found outlet in burying their dead in passage-graves, were established in Brittany three thousand five hundred years before the birth of Christ. Pushing slowly up the Irish Sea they arrived in Wales and in eastern Ireland about five hundred years later. The estuary of the Boyne may well have been their first entry point, because the earliest site at which they have been recognised in Ireland is at Townley Hall, less than one mile from the point in the valley of the Boyne to which the tides of the estuary flow. Here Professor Eogan and I excavated a simple passage-grave whose stones were without decoration; underneath the tomb there was an occupation-site probably with small huts which was dated by radiocarbon to about two thousand seven hundred years before Christ. That the occupants were farmers there was no doubt because many charred cereal grains were recovered from the debris in the hearths. The charcoal in the hearths came not from forest trees such as oak and elm, but from bushes, hazel, hawthorn, willow and mountain ash, which would have been growing in hedges and abandoned fields. This shows that the farmers had already swept away the original woodlands in the course of their operations.

The lands round the Boyne are among the most fertile in Ireland, and the grasslands of Meath have long been famous for their power in the fattening of cattle, and here the builders of megalithic tombs grew in wealth and in numbers. Social organisation must have grown also, and leaders must have emerged who had control of, if they did not personally own, the accumulating wealth of the community. Increased numbers led to a demand for more tombs, and three ridge-tops, known to us today as Dowth, Newgrange and Knowth, were developed as cemetery sites and at these clusters of small passage-graves were erected. The building of such tombs must by now have been becoming a routine task, and specialist gangs of builders will have emerged, occupied full-time on the construction of tombs. These men had no time in which to take part in food-production, and must have been supported by the food-surplus built up by the community. In other words they were wage-earners, probably the first in Ireland.

By this time the food-surplus or accumulated wealth of the community must have been very considerable, because it became possible to contemplate building a few very large and very sophisticated tombs instead of the numerous small ones that had served hitherto. Such an accumulation of wealth can only have been built up by a very large farming population. Just how big was the group? Estimating the size of early populations is a very hazardous task, but Professor Herity has suggested that there must have been a population of about four thousand people living under almost urban conditions in camps or barracks and carrying out large-scale or collective farming operations. Who was in control of the group? If there were kings, at least in death we would expect to have seen them set apart from the rest of the people and buried, as were the contemporary Pharoahs of Egypt, in royal pomp. But many seasons of excavation in the Boyne valley have produced no trace of any royal burials. Does the emphasis on death that we can identify by excavation imply also an emphasis on re-birth which we can never hope to find by digging? The axial line of the passage in the great tomb below the mound at Newgrange points to the spot where at the December solstice the dying sun of winter ceases to fall and starts again to rise to the promise of spring. The community must have been permeated with religious fervour; was it like other primitive societies under the control of a self-perpetuating college of priests?

That there was both wealth and control is certain. How else could the mound at Newgrange, built of two hundred thousand tonnes of earth and stone, many of the stones weighing more than one tonne each, have sprung into existence? Professor O'Kelly, whose recent death we all regret, had at the end of thirteen years of work at Newgrange no doubts on the matter; he wrote 'the whole undertaking was carefully thought out and planned from first to last and carried out with something like military precision'. These sentiments are readily echoed by Professor Eogan who has already spent twenty years trying to unravel the secrets of the sister mound at Knowth.

The great Irish passage-graves did not merely grow in size; they grew in sophistication also. The passage grew longer; the chamber added side-chambers necessitating a much more complex roof; the stones in the kerb got bigger; many new motifs were added to the inscribed ornamental designs, and the designs were much more lavishly applied, invading the stones of the passage and the roof of the chamber and splaying out over the stones in the kerb.

For almost three centuries now archaeologists and artists have been intrigued by the abstract ornamentation of the tombs. Many of the designs recur over and over again, just as the letters of the alphabet recur in written words. To the Neolithic peasants who frequented the tombs they must have served as letters capable of being assembled to convey a message, most probably a religious message of some kind. Painstaking scholarship has deciphered many ancient languages even though they were written or carved in strange characters; can we hope one day to read the message of these Neolithic stones?

But let us return to the building of the monuments. The proportions and the design of the chamber and passage had to be decided on by accomplished architects who were aware of the weights and pressures that the stones employed would have to bear, if the whole structure were not to collapse. The circumference and height of the enveloping mound was next considered so as to know how many kerb-stones to order and how much stone and earth to bring to the site.

Professor O'Kelly pictured the whole operation as too complex for a single work-force, and he envisaged the work being distributed among specialist gangs. The humblest group were the drawers of stone and earth for the body of the mound, the most sophisticated were the artists decorating the stones. Skilled structural erectors set up the stonework, and specialist geologists sought out the large stones necessary for the chamber and the kerb. This group had also to go further afield for special stones for decorative rather than structural purposes. The recent reconstruction of the entrance facade at Newgrange has made it clear to all that white quartz was used for decoration in this area. At Knowth also the entrance areas have a quantity of white quartz. Much of this quartz must have been carried for quite a distance. Oval boulders of granite, about the size of a football, are also common at the entrance areas both at Newgrange and Knowth; these do not occur locally, but can be collected on the north shore of Dundalk Bay, at a distance of about twenty miles from the Boyne monuments, though of course these stones could have been transported by boat. Professor Eogan's work at Knowth is revealing other collections of stones, again foreign to the neighbourhood.

While it is just conceivable that one day we may be able to understand the message that the decorated stones are trying to convey to us, it is probably too much to hope that we will ever know what special significance the tomb-builders must have attached to these stones, which were specially imported and arranged in patterns. But significance there must have been, else why spend so much skill and time in their collection?

Among many other unanswered questions, one major one must stand out. What can the size of the community have been, and over what area did their farming activities extend, if three enormous monuments were required, although each was capable of holding many hundreds of burials and was separated from its neighbours by a distance of no more than one mile? There is no reason to think that they were not all in use simultaneously, and they seem to have been erected about two thousand five hundred years before the birth of Christ, only two hundred years after the first arrival of the simple passage-grave in the Boyne Valley.

I should have made it clear before, and do so now, that the combined length of the passage and the chamber never reaches the centre of the great mound that buries them. There is thus no reason why the mound should not contain more than one tomb; in fact there is probably room for about six if they were carefully arranged. We now know that at Knowth there are two tombs more or less back to back in the mound. When this fact came to light Professor O'Kelly made a special effort at Newgrange to see if it also could hold two chambers, but without success. Dowth has one large tomb, and also a much smaller structure which may or may not be a passage-grave. If we build an elongated mound, and not a round one, then there is no limit to the number of tombs we can put inside it. In Brittany, probably the ancestral home of the Irish passage-grave, we have such a mound with no less than eleven tombs side by side within it. There was thus no ideological objection to having more than one tomb in a mound, and Knowth has at least two. So why was it necessary in the Boyne valley to build three enormous mounds holding only four tombs between them when one mound holding four tombs would have provided the same accommodation?

Erskine Childers Senior wrote a brilliant book called *The Riddle of the Sands*; I can only say that after three hundred years of inspection and one hundred and fifty years of excavation the great tombs of the Boyne Valley still hold many riddles for us to solve.

In heroic Irish lore they appear as Brú na Bóinne, the homes on the Boyne of mythological gods and kings. I prefer to regard them as temples, the temples that almost five thousand years ago served the first community to rise to importance in Ireland.

Professor O'Kelly saw the tombs as temples as he tells us

in his summing-up. 'The building of Newgrange and of the two other equally imposing mounds of Knowth and Dowth, all within a few kilometres of one another, cannot be regarded as other than the expression of some powerful force or motivation, brought to the extremes of aggrandisement in these three monuments, the cathedrals of megalithic religion.' Professor Herity's assessment is similar. 'Here in the Boyne valley these Passage Grave Builders established a powerful economy and constructed massive tumuli which, in the elegance of their structural and artistic features, reveal their builders' sophistication and the richness and maturity of the culture they established in Ireland.'

We can never know exactly how that cultural group was organised. The tombs by their massive construction, by the architectural principles on which they were erected and by their religious purpose of caring for the remains of the dead, tell us more clearly than any words that this first Irish community was both purposeful and sophisticated.

2. The Coming of Christianity

Liam de Paor

It must be regarded as remarkable that once a year, in cities all over the modern world, a fifth-century British bishop is celebrated. It is not St Ambrose, or St Jerome, or St Augustine of the patriarchal age of the Christian church who has achieved this long posthumous distinction; but St Patrick, whose contributions to theology and literature were a great deal less than any of these. Why? Undoubtedly, in part, because the descendants of the people among whom he worked have themselves become a dispersed part of the English-speaking world – among the nations that have dominated the last two centuries of world history. British history in the fifth century is obscure in the extreme, and indeed were it not for the writings of this man Patrick we would have a great deal less understanding of it than we have. He is the first British person in history that we can come to know. To know *about* him is another matter, and to know about the movement of which he was a part is another matter still.

Because of the inadequacies of the written source materials there have for centuries been controversies among scholars and others about Patrick and the conversion of Ireland. The main questions seemed to be resolved when at the beginning of this century the eminent historian of the Roman empire, Bury, produced a study of the life of St Patrick and his place in history. Bury was immensely learned in the historical materials of the later Roman empire; not, however, in materials relating to early Ireland. But his synthesis, as it happened, was highly acceptable to nationalist and Catholic Ireland at the turn of the century. His job of journeywork on the Patrician material came to be not merely accepted but defended tooth-and-nail as the true traditional history of the great missionary.

But, just over forty years ago, old doubts were renewed. In 1942 O'Rahilly attempted to demolish the Bury thesis in a lecture given to the Dublin Institute for Advanced Studies under the title 'The Two Patricks'. This stimulated a frenzy of investigation of the Patrician problem. Things are calm again now. O'Rahilly's own conclusions have not stood the test, except in part, but his demolition of the Bury synthesis remains effective. What has happened, as so often happens in scholarly questions of this kind is that we now know a great deal more about our sources and about the whole context of the problem, but a good deal of legendary embellishment of St Patrick's story has been cut away. We appreciate now that the Irish and Welsh annals are unreliable before about the middle of the sixth century – since they were constructs, or at best attempted reconstructions, which were done much later than this. We appreciate that the seventh-century accounts of Patrick's life, written at least two hundred years after the events they purport to describe, are far from being summaries of a carefully preserved tradition. On the contrary, they are propagandist tracts motivated by seventh-century controversies and embodying much folklore material of a standard type into which the name of Patrick has been borrowed. We must fall back on what we can learn from contemporary sources – including St Patrick's own writings – from the careful criticism of later documents, from archaeology, inscriptions, placenames and other types of information. If this strips the story of Ireland's conversion of much picturesque and legendary narrative, it also deepens our understanding. We can see, for example, that Ireland was not converted overnight by one man – St Patrick (whose work indeed was probably confined to a part of Ulster and a part of north Connacht) – although he emerges as a much more credible, much more human, and, in the long run, a much more remarkable figure.

Patrick's own writings, or those that have survived, are two in number. They are both in the form of letters. One, the earlier as is generally believed, is addressed to the soldiers of a British prince whom Patrick calls Coroticus – giving a latinised form to a name which is elsewhere given the form Caradoc. Caradoc, a Christian, at least nominally, had carried out a raid in which his soldiers carried off a number of Patrick's newly converted Christians as slaves and had sold them to the pagan Picts of Scotland. Patrick protests, denounces this crime, excommunicates Caradoc, and demands the return of the captives. The other work, longer and later in date, is generally known as the *Confession*. In it Patrick primarily addresses some British clergymen, defending his mission to them against criticism and affirming that he had been chosen by God to do his work, although unworthy and uneducated. These may seem very meagre documents for the study of a major event in the history of Ireland, but they shine like a beacon in the general darkness of the fifth century. This is a time when not only the hitherto pagan and still largely unlettered island of Ireland is without records, but the long Romanised island of Great Britain has also lapsed into the obscurity which characterises the end of Roman imperial rule in the west.

Let us begin then by summarising what we know about the situation. Britain, twice invaded in large-scale raids by Julius Caesar in the first century BC, was successfuly invaded by Roman armies under the emperor Claudius in the middle of the first century AD. Roman rule was established as far north, approximately, as the line of the present English-Scottish border. For most of the centuries of the occupation the effective frontier was Hadrian's Wall, running from the present city of Carlisle to the city of Newcastle. The northern part of the Roman province was predominantly military in character, with its capital at the old Celtic city of York, while the south-eastern part of Britain was peaceful, civilian and assimilated into the general polity of the western empire. In the late first century the addition of the neighbouring island of Ireland to the empire was contemplated. Agricola, then governor of Britain, carried out reconnaissance and assembled forces on the British shore opposite Ireland's east coast; but he subsequently changed his mind.

If this series could include non-events, there might well have been an essay on the Roman decision *not* to invade Ireland – perhaps the most important non-event in our history, since it separates our island's experience, in a very important matter, from that of most of western Europe. However, the information obtained by Agricola's reconnaissance is now thought to be the main basis of the account of Ireland given by the geographer Ptolemy in the second century. This describes a country inhabited by people whose tribal and place names are Celtic.

Most of the inhabitants of Britain were also Celtic-speaking at the time of the Roman invasion. Christianity was introduced to Roman Britain probably chiefly by traders, but we know next to nothing of its early history. Research has shown that Roman religions were chiefly spread along and from the Mediterranean by traders who took their gods with them – but soldiers, travellers and even slaves played a large part. The Persian religion, Mithraism, spread along the trade routes and military frontiers in the late second and early third centuries and was in the words of W. H. C. Frend 'a world religion in the making'. This remained the dominant religion of the Roman garrison in Britain down to the end of the empire. By the same route spread the cults of Isis, Serapis and Jupiter Dolichenus. The spread of Christianity was additionally aided by the Jewish communities of the Diaspora. In the second century wherever there were Jewish communities there were also Christians. While in the west – outside Rome and some of the larger towns of Africa – there were comparatively few Jewish settlements, the cities of Lyons and Vienne were exceptional. These were on the main trade routes leading north from Marseilles, and most of the Christians there apparently belonged to trading groups of Asia Minor. It may be from there that Christianity was established in western Britain: the traditions of early British martyrs include the names of Aaron and Julius beheaded in Caerleon-on-Usk, possibly in the same persecution in which the soldier St Alban met his death in Verulamium, north of London.

There were traditions of very early Christianity at Glastonbury, and these are now supported by the evidence of archaeology. This was a centre of high pre-Roman culture, and some of the finest specimens of Celtic art have come from the nearby lake villages. It may be that Christianity reached the West Country and the southern Irish Sea virtually independently of the Roman system, at a very early date – the Christian message may have reached Wexford or Cork centuries before St Patrick: we simply do not know.

Our earliest documentary evidence comes from Tertullian,

writing in North Africa in about AD 200. Origen, about 240, wrote that Christianity was a unifying force among the Britons – whatever that may mean. It is just possible that when Constantine was declared emperor – which occurred at York in 306 – he may already have personally adopted Christianity. In 314 three British bishops attended the council at Arles, and in 359 a number of British bishops attended the council at Rimini. In the doctrinal controversies of the fourth century both Chrysostom and Jerome declared the orthodoxy of the British church, but about AD 400 Victricius of Rouen came to settle some quarrel among the British bishops. Victricius was an important figure: an enthusiast for the new monastic movement just reaching the west from the east Mediterranean.

By about 410 we have clear evidence that Britain was the nursery of a doctrine, concerning divine grace and free-will, which was powerfully opposed by the orthodox. This is known as Pelagianism, from its originator Pelagius. Although he was British he is described by St Jerome, who wanted to emphasise the barbarism of his background, as being 'stuffed with Irish porridge'. But he brought his teaching to Rome and the east. Concern obviously grew about the state of British Christianity. The British church was a protegé of the church in Gaul. St Germanus of Auxerre appears to have reported to Rome on the spread of heresy in Britain. The scanty sources are ambiguous, but it seems probable that the Palladius who was involved in these matters was a deacon of the church of Auxerre, sent with this report to Rome. In 429, at any rate, the Bishop of Rome sent Germanus of Auxerre and Lupus of Troyes to win Britain back to orthodoxy. This bishop, Pope Celestine, was a strong opponent of Pelagianism. He was also, it seems, unenthusiastic about monasticism. It was he who, in 431, sent Palladius to the Irish Christians as their first bishop.

We know this from the chronicle of Prosper of Acquitaine, a controversialist who took the orthodox side on the Pelagian question. Elsewhere Prosper writes about the mission of Palladius that Pope Celestine 'ordaining a bishop for the Irish at once worked to keep the Roman island Catholic and to make the barbarian island Christian'. This official extension of the formal organisation of the church to Ireland in the person of the bishop Palladius is the earliest dated event in our history.

I might add here in parenthesis that the commonly accepted date of 432 for the coming of St Patrick is worthless. The Irish writers of the seventh and eighth centuries, possessing the evidence of Prosper's chronicle with the 431 date for Palladius (about whom they knew nothing) and believing that St Patrick *must* have arrived very soon after, devised a stylised chronology: 431 Palladius arrives; 432 Patrick arrives; 433 Ireland is converted *by St Patrick*.

Britain's troubles at the end of the fourth century were not only, or mainly, ecclesiastical. The major problems encountered by the empire in general were met in full measure in this, its most remote westerly province. Like other parts of the west, the province had long been subject to barbarian attack. Some time about the middle of the fourth century the country was still in good shape, but in AD 367, if not earlier, the raids from outside were beginning to have severe effects. In that year there occurred what Ammianus Marcellinus calls 'a barbarian conspiracy': the Picts, Irish and Attacotti stormed Hadrian's Wall, aided by some disaffected garrison troops, while simultaneously Saxons from across the North Sea and Franks from east of the Rhine invaded south-eastern England. The emperor, Valentinian I, the following year sent troops to retrieve the province: their general, Theodosius, had to relieve a siege of London. But it is doubtful if things in Britain ever returned to what, in earlier Roman terms, might be called 'normal'.

After the 'conspiracy' of 367, there were many further incursions, and the organisation of the Roman province began to fall to pieces. In the 380s, the army in Britain proclaimed their general Magnus Maximus emperor, and in his bid for power he took the legions out of the province. He was by no means the first, in this province which had become noted for military disaffection, to be so proclaimed, but his defection marks the beginning of the end of Roman Britain. Government continued, but with increasingly inadequate forces, who had to defend a very long coastline against the Saxons on one side and the Irish on the other; while it seems that the wall which had marked the defence zone against the Picts fell into disrepair. Then came the crisis of the western empire. On New Year's Eve, 406, the Alans, Vandals and

Sueves crossed the frozen Rhine at Mainz and poured into Gaul in an irresistible invasion. During 407 no less than three emperors were proclaimed in Britain, two of them being murdered almost immediately after their exaltation. The third rallied to himself the regular army and took it to Gaul, to pursue his imperial ambition. Britain, denuded of regular troops, was attacked again most severely by a major Saxon raid. Rome itself, in 410, was sacked by Alaric and his Goths – an event which was traumatic in its effects on the minds of the imperial élite in every province of the empire. The Romanised Britons, proud of their Roman heritage by now, but despairing of the Roman administration, decided to go it alone, to defend themselves and re-organise their province, on continuing Roman lines but with local rather than Roman control.

Somewhere in this context we must place the effort to recover Britain from Pelagianism, already discussed – and we must place Patrick. St Patrick was a Briton: there is no doubt whatever about that: he gives us the information himself several times. He came from the rural gentry of Roman Britain; again he leaves us in no doubt about either his original social status or his Roman-ness. His father, Calpornius, was both a *decurio* and a deacon, owned a *villula*, or estate, and employed a sizeable staff. Patrick's grandfather, Potitus, had been a priest. Since, to judge by Patrick's account of his childhood, the household was not a particularly pious one, it is possible that Calpornius had received the order of deacon in order to be exempt, as a clerk in holy orders, from the tax obligations of the class of *curiales*. Patrick gives us the name of the neighbouring town, but the placename appears to have been garbled in the course of manuscript copying and it cannot be identified with certainty. The balance of probability – helped by recent work – would suggest somewhere near Carlisle. At any rate Patrick's home life came to an abrupt end in his sixteenth year. A large-scale Irish raid swept through the countryside where his parents' home lay, sweeping up many young captives of both sexes – Patrick speaks of 'thousands' – including members of Calpornius's family and household. The boy was brought to Ireland, a slave, and worked in servitude as a herd. Later legend has fixed on

Slemish, in Antrim, as the place of his captivity, but there is good reason for doubting this. Patrick himself clearly implies that the place was 'the wood of Foclut, by the western sea' – which was just north of the present-day Killala, in Mayo.

Here he underwent some sort of conversion, had dreams and visions, after six years escaped, and after further dreams and visions (when he had returned home) determined to come back. How he proceeded to fulfil this vocation we do not know with any precision. There was some sort of rudimentary diocesan organisation in Britain by the fifth century, and there were Christians outside as well as inside the frontiers. It appears that some time about the beginning of the century a bishop had been appointed to work north of the wall. This man, St Ninia, had established his church at *Candida Casa*, now Whithorn in Galloway, and was credited with the evangelising from there of the southern Picts. His home base was probably Carlisle, the chief Roman centre in this frontier country. Carlisle, although formally classified not as a city but as a mere town – *vicus* – appears to have had a full urban organisation, including a bishop. This was possibly Patrick's base too. What seems clear is that some group or organisation of British ecclesiastics supported Patrick's mission – although with misgivings. His asset was a powerful sense of vocation; but he lacked the education normally considered necessary for a bishop at that time. His education, you will remember, had been rudely interrupted at the age of sixteen. Yet in the long run he was, as he put it himself, 'constituted' bishop in Ireland. The normal, and indeed the required, practice of the time was that a bishop was consecrated and sent only to an already existing Christian community – one, furthermore, which had actually asked for a bishop. So Palladius, Ireland's first bishop, was sent, not to the heathen, but to 'the Irish Christians'.

So we must turn back to Ireland. The country was densely wooded, with some cultivated clearings, stretches of upland pasture, and vast tracts of empty bogland. It still continued the way of life of the prehistoric early Iron Age of western Europe. A cattle-owning aristocracy – with a life-stye in some ways comparable to that of the Masai or the Zulu of a century or so ago – was organised in tribal groupings under chiefs (the term they used was *rí*) and under great overlords, or high-kings, who enjoyed a vague and intermittent hegemony. There were several major tribal groupings, which we may term, in the old sense of the word, 'nations'. The most important of these was that of the *Ulaid*, the people of the north, whose approximate southern boundaries were the valleys of Erne and Boyne. Other major groups included the *Lagin* of eastern and central Ireland. Some sub-groups of these tribal nations were vigorously colonising overseas in parts of western Britain – Cornwall, Wales, the Isle of Man, and parts of western Scotland. There was almost certainly a considerable British admixture among the Irish of the north-east. It seems not unlikely that Christians were sufficiently numerous in this corner of Ireland to require a bishop. Patrick, however, to judge from his writings, seems to have had a special ambition, or vocation, to preach the Gospel in the remote pagan west.

We cannot, however, reconstruct the schedule of his life in Ireland. His *Confession* is an outpouring of thanks and praise for what had been achieved through him, of protestations – to his accusers or inquisitors in Britain – of the propriety of his conduct as a missionary, of the revelations he had experienced in visions. It is a disconnected narrative, breaking off in a bewildering way in the middle of a story to recount some other experience which has come to mind; expressed with difficulty in a rusty Latin language; but above all concerned with internal rather than external experience. Patrick has often been, and continues at the time of writing to be, in danger; he has been taken captive and chained. He has baptised thousands, of all classes: he mentions the sons and daughters of petty kings; he mentions the women of high degree whose gifts of jewellery laid upon the church altars he has returned; he also mentions the special difficulties encountered by slave-women he had baptised. He refers to 'monks and virgins of Christ' – but it is unlikely that these were in organised communities; more likely, rather, that he had drafted rules for those who wished to practise monastic discipline in private. He estimates the amount he has spent on his mission: the price of fifteen slaves. Much of this was spent on safe-conducts; and he seems to have been required, for his own safety or that of his retinue, to 'hire', as it were, the service of kings' sons as travel companions: 'protection money'. Several times he emphasises what he considers a remarkable feature of his mission – and what probably initiated the great growth of his later reputation: this is that he had been to the ends of the earth, preaching the gospel where no one had been before him to baptise or to ordain. Now, he would not consider this remarkable if he were the first or the only missionary to the Irish.

When Patrick wrote the letter against the soldiers of Coroticus he was almost certainly in north-east Ireland, perhaps at Down, possibly in Armagh. The Caradoc or Ceredic in question, it seems most probable, was ruler of Strathclyde. This Ceredic's date, which cannot be established with precision, was in the middle years of the fifth century. Patrick's references to the remote ends of the earth cannot be to his stay in Armagh and Down. I think we can take it that he is here referring to the fulfilment of his mission to return to those who lived beside the forest of Foclut.

In the late seventh century, more than two hundred years after the event, Bishop Tírechán, in pursuing controversial claims to church rents and jurisdiction, tried to reconstruct Patrick's journeys. He first of all brings him to Brega, in the east, using the already developed saga of Patrick's confrontation on Tara with the druids of a high king. This is unhistorical: it is an old myth-tale long antedating Christianity. Then he brings him to the upper Shannon, consecrating bishops such as Mel at Ardagh or encountering traces of earlier bishops, such as Sacellus at Basilica Sanctorum. Then he brings him to the far west, to the Moy country: and the tales he collects here are free from traces of the activities of other missionaries. Patrick may well indeed be the founder of the 'Great Church of the Moy', on the outskirts of Ballina, and this may well be the scene of that part of his mission that he thought most remarkable. The later narratives and other documents associated numbers of Gaulish and British bishops with him – notably Auxilius, Secundinus, Iserninus and Benignus. But it is clear from Patrick's own words that he was working, episcopally speaking, alone. He was the pioneer who went deep into the bush.

The whole south of Ireland received its Christianity from other hands. Even at the time when Armagh and the Patrick legend were claiming all Ireland, in the seventh, eighth and ninth centuries, this was tenaciously remembered. Ailbhe, Ibhar, Ciaran, Declan and others in the south are presented in the tradition as *pre*-Patrician. Kildare attempted, down to the end of the seventh century, to establish the primacy for itself. Auxilius, Secundinus and Iserninus are associated with the east midlands and were probably the first systematic organisers of the church there. Lommanus's church at Trim is admitted, even by the *Book of Armagh,* to have been founded thirty years before Armagh itself.

Apart from its intrinsic significance and importance, the conversion can be seen as part of a Romanising process which was very marked at least from the third century onwards. For the peoples outside its frontiers the Roman empire had enormous prestige. For several centuries the Irish ruling classes copied Roman fashions and styles; and they were familiar with Roman civilisation through trade, through their raids on the imperial provinces, and perhaps through mercenary military service. There is no way of knowing how long there had been Christians, even Christian communities, in Ireland before the church made its great organisational drive in the fifth century.

All the evidence goes to show that as the military and administrative structures of the western Roman empire collapsed, more and more responsibility passed into the hands of the Christian bishops, themselves in the Roman provinces chiefly drawn from the administrative and ruling classes. They continued to expand *their* kingdom, while the earthly kingdom fell to pieces around them: they took heed of St Augustine's words. Ireland, whose conquest had not been undertaken by the Roman legions, was brought into the empire of the Roman church at this time – not by St Patrick alone, or even chiefly by St Patrick, but by scores of bishops following in the footsteps of Palladius. Patrick was outstanding, but he was not alone. Between them, the bishops of that distant time both transformed Ireland's relations with Europe at a most critical period and gave a beginning to the one major force that has continuously animated our history for the past fifteen hundred years.

3. Brian Boru and the Battle of Clontarf

Donnchadh Ó Corráin

When most people think about Brian Boru they think about Vikings and it may be as well to talk a little about them first. Now if you were a Viking off the coast of Rathlin in 795 you might like to know what sort of country you were coming to and how it might differ from your own. The answer is, putting climate and Christianity aside (and that is a lot to put aside), Ireland would have been much like the one you came from, a country of fragmented political power, local lordship and powerful kings attempting to establish rule over large areas. The dominant dynasty in Ireland was that of the Uí Néill, divided into two great branches, one in the North with its power centre in mid-Ulster and the other in the South with its power centre in the rich lands of Meath. The Uí Néill were busy on the eve of the Viking attack (and indeed in the early years of it) trying to smash the power of the Leinster kings and extend their political authority southwards. Munster and Connacht lay outside the area of their authority. Nowhere was there a national monarchy or a recognised national centre of power. That lay in the future in Ireland, as it did in Norway, where most of the Vikings who were to get involved with Ireland were, in fact, to come from.

Perhaps the most striking difference between Viking and Irish society was Christianity. The Irish churches, most of them great monastic centres, like Armagh, Clonmacnoise, Cork, Clonard and so on, were rich and powerful, and in a sense corrupt, if by corrupt one means worldly. They were ruled by great dynasties of hereditary abbots and clergy and these very often were closely related to the secular rulers of the kingdom in which they stood, as in Armagh, which first encountered the Vikings as a monastic aggressor. The Vikings had plundered a coastal monastery dependent on Armagh, and

the head church evidently sent out a search-and-destroy
mission, which got a bloody nose. Armagh was ruled by
hereditary clergy closely related to the local ruling dynasty,
and the same was true of many of the great monasteries all
over Ireland. The Vikings, then, fell on no innocent monkdom
but on great and rich centres with long experience of violence.
The monasteries were regularly sacked in wars between the
Irish kingdoms, and when the Anglo-Saxons raided eastern
Meath in 684 they, too, plundered the monasteries. These
monasteries were the centres of the most advanced economic
development. They were rich in treasure because of their own
extensive lands – and it is difficult for us to imagine how great
a landowner the Church was in the early middle ages. They
were rich, too, because of the offerings of the faithful and
because the people used the churches as a kind of safe deposit
box. They were ripe, then, for the picking.

In the very end of the eighth century the first Vikings
appeared off the Irish coast at almost exactly the same time as
they appeared off England. Their first recorded raid was on
Rathlin Island in 795 – natural enough, for it was directly on
their way southwards into the Irish sea. Iona was attacked in
802 and again in 806, and in 807 the Community of Iona began
to build a new monastery in Kells, Co. Meath, inland and
safe, or so they thought, from the Vikings. Now the raiders
appeared on the west coast. They raided Inishmurray off the
Sligo coast in 807. They appeared in Galway Bay in the same
year and sacked the little monastery of Roscam at the very
head of Galway Bay, a little to the west of Oranmore. In 812
and 813 they were in the wilds of Mayo and in Connemara
and in 824 they plundered Skellig off the Kerry coast. Until
the middle of the 830s these were hit-and-run affairs. The
Vikings appeared swiftly in small sea-borne and fast-moving
groups and disappeared just as quickly, and they rarely went
more than twenty miles inland. They were difficult to deal
with as an enemy because they had the advantage of speed
and surprise, but they did not always get away with it. The
Ulstermen slaughtered them in 811, and in 812 the men of
Kerry and Mayo had some success against them. But from
830 the raids became more intense, as they did in England and
in continental Europe and they began to plunder the heartland

of major Irish kingdoms. Yet the Irish held out more doggedly than any other west European country. Eventually, the Vikings wrested the rich duchy of Normandy from the French kings, and they over-ran and ruled all England except for the kingdom of Wessex, but they won no great territories in Ireland – and not because the Irish were united. Indeed, the Irish were more concerned with fighting one another than with fighting the Vikings, and there was certainly no national resistence in any modern sense of the word.

The Vikings pushed up the Shannon, the Bann, the Boyne and the Erne, and in the winter of 840 and 841 they put their fleet in Lough Neagh safe for the winter. Next winter they spent in Dublin. About 845 things looked black for the Irish kings: the Vikings were raiding and plundering in the very heart of Ireland. The abbot of Armagh, the principal ecclesiastic in Ireland, was captured by them and carried off to the ships. He was ransomed some time later, little the worse for the wear. Most of you will have heard in school of the super-Viking Turgesius who was said to have captured Armagh and expelled the abbot, and to have taken the abbacy for himself. His pagan wife Ota is said to have given pagan oracles from the high altar at Clonmacnoise and the story goes that he was well on his way to conquering Ireland when Malachy I captured him and drowned him in Lough Owel. There is little truth in the tale. Turgesius did indeed exist but he was only one of many Viking leaders active in the Shannon area. For the rest, the story is political propaganda put about by the O'Briens in the twelfth century to blacken the Uí Néill and to show how they were no good at defending the Church and Ireland from the Vikings, unlike their own great ancestor, Brian Boru, who did the heroic thing at the battle of Clontarf.

By the 850s the first great period of Viking raids was over. The Viking settlement of Dublin remained, holding the status of any Irish petty kingdom, and the Irish kings went on with what was their principal business all the time, building up and consolidating their own provincial power bases and fighting with one another for dominance over the whole country. It was in the course of these struggles that the family of Brian Boru first came into prominence. Munster was ruled by the Eoganacht but they had their difficulties, and one of the principal ones was the bitter hostility of the Uí Néill who were most anxious to extend their power into Munster. The rulers of Munster did produce some remarkable kings but in the 850s they, too, were forced to submit to the Uí Néill. There was a second great period of Viking activity in Ireland. It began in 914 because opportunities for Viking raiders were becoming scarce in Europe and in England, and they had another go at Ireland. This time they seemed to have concentrated their attack on the south of Ireland. The Viking towns of Waterford, Cork and Limerick date from this period, and the kings of Munster seemed to have made a bad job of defending themselves. Elsewhere, in the north and the west and in the midlands, the Irish counterattacked with great success. The last great Eoganacht king of Cashel and of Munster was Cormac mac Cuilennáin. He was killed fighting the Leinstermen in 908, and after that the power of the kings of Munster withered away. Meanwhile, in the west of Munster, straddling the very strategic waterway of the Shannon, and close to the Viking city of Limerick a new dynasty, the Dál gCais, were building themselves a firm power-base. This new dynasty came of quite humble origins, the Déisi (meaning subject people), and their original home was in east Limerick in the barony of Small County. But like many who rise in the world they shook off their humble associations and called themselves Dál gCais, a name invented for them by their genealogists, and they gave themselves an ancestry as noble as any of their Eoganacht predecessors.

They expanded into Clare at an early period and by the middle of the tenth century they had become a power to be reckoned with in Munster politics. Ironically, they owed much to the Vikings, for the Vikings did a lot to destroy the power of their predecessors. It was the Vikings who made the Irish aware of naval power and, when navies were important, dominance over the Shannon estuary was a big strategic advantage. By the 950s we find the Dál gCais doing battle with the Eoganacht kings of Munster and the Uí Néill, and when their king Cennétig died in 951 the annals called him king of Thomond and claimant to the kingship of Munster. His sons were to go much further and much faster. In the 960s Mathgamain, son of Cennétig, was one of the two principal claimants to the kingship of Munster. The other was Mael Muad mac Brain of the branch of the Eoganacht settled about Bandon. The two, naturally, were bitter enemies. Mael Muad allied himself with the Vikings of Limerick and with some local Munster rulers and met Mathgamain in battle at Solohead – where Limerick Junction now is – and Mathgamain defeated his opponents. And on the following day he attacked and sacked the Viking city of Limerick. Later O'Brien propagandists made out that this was an unholy alliance of Irish traitors and Viking baddies, but this was simply the normal type of struggle in tenth-century Ireland. Mathgamain later expelled the Viking ruler of Limerick and by the 970s he was one of the dominant rulers in Munster. In 976, however, his enemies got together, captured him and murdered him. It did them little good. He was succeeded by his brother Brian who brought the fortunes of the Dál gCais to a new height, toppled the Uí Néill, and in one sense at least made the kingship of Ireland a prize worth fighting for. It is important to remember that by the time Brian became king of Munster the Viking wars were effectively over.

The Vikings have been called many things: unprincipled blackguards, pagans filled with hostility to Christianity, plunderers of churches and shrines. They certainly plundered monasteries, but so did the Irish. They were not much interested in religion and it has been said (with some truth) that the Scandinavians came late to Christianity and left early. At any rate, those in Ireland, even in the late ninth century, seemed to have adopted Christianity rather rapidly. They have been blamed for the decay of the Irish Church, hereditary monasteries, non-celibate clergy and a decline in learning. But there were hereditary monasteries in Ireland long before the first Viking ever set foot in the place and celibacy, until recent times, was never the strong suit of the Irish clergy. It is perhaps a telling fact that in the first twenty-five years of the Viking war the annals attribute twenty-six acts of violence to the Vikings and eighty-seven to the Irish themselves. It is quite wrong, therefore, to think that Brian Boru became king of Muster at a time when Ireland was ravaged by Viking raids, a land of empty ruined churches and burnt libraries. Even at their height the Viking wars were nothing as intense as that and if you met a fully armed Viking intent on mayhem once in your life, as an Irishman of the tenth century, you were probably a bit unlucky.

By the time of Brian the Vikings had become traders and entrepreneurs. There is a difference between these, but it may not be all that much. By the tenth century the Vikings had for the most part become town dwellers and merchants. O'Brien political propaganda, and there was a lot of it, put out long after the Viking wars, when indeed these wars were only a vague and heroic memory, painted a lurid picture of Viking tyranny over Ireland. Of course, there is no basis for this. Neither is there any basis for the story that from his earliest years Brian was a determined leader of the resistance and an outstanding guerrilla fighter in the hills of east Clare who fought on until his forces were reduced to a handful. This is the invention of storytellers.

On Mathgamain's death, he succeeded to the kingship and immediately rounded on his brother's killers. In 977 he attacked the Vikings of Limerick. Their king Imar and his two sons, all Christians, fled for refuge to the monastery of Inis Cathaig (Scattery Island) and Brian desecrated the monastery and killed them in the sanctuary. In the next year he defeated the remainder of the coalition that had killed Mathgamain. From now on Brian's rise to power was phenomenal.

Limerick and Munster were now in his hands. In 980 he first encountered the hostility of the Uí Néill when he attempted to dominate Ossory, roughly the present Co. Kilkenny. Brian put fleets on the Shannon, he attacked Connacht, and his troops penetrated as far north as Cavan. In 984 he allied with the Vikings of Waterford, as he needed their fleet, and planned an attack on Leinster. When he carried it out the Viking fleet plundered the coastline of south Leinster and Brian brought fire and sword inland ravaging fortresses, monasteries and territories. In the 980s he tightened his grip on Munster and took the hostages of the monastic cities of Lismore, Cork and Emly. All this was in preparation for an all out effort against the Uí Néill, now ruled by their great king Malachy II. By 997 Malachy was forced militarily by Brian to meet him in conference at Clonfert. There they

partitioned Ireland between them and Brian was recognised
as master of the southern half of the country. This, of course,
made him ruler of Leinster, and the Leinstermen resented rule
by Brian as much, perhaps even more, than they resented the
attacks of the Uí Néill. Leinster revolted and joined with the
Vikings of Dublin in that revolt. Brian dealt with it swiftly
and effectively, and in 999 at the battle of Glenn Máma the
Leinstermen and their Viking allies were decisively defeated.
But Brian followed up this by attacking Dublin. He spent the
following January to the beginning of February in Dublin. He
plundered the city for booty, burned the fortress and expelled
Sitric, the king of Dublin, Eventually Sitric, who had nowhere to go anyway, submitted to Brian who appointed
him king of Dublin under his authority. Now the time had
come for Brian to break his agreement with Malachy.

He set out to establish his authority over the whole country
and in this attempt he was consistently supported by the
Vikings of Dublin. He led a number of expeditions into the
North; one in 1001 rapidly followed by another in 1002, when
Malachy himself was forced to submit to Brian. He marched
north in 1004, and again in 1005. On this occasion he remained
at Armagh for a whole week, placed 20 ounces of gold on the
high altar and had his inscription entered in the *Book of Armagh*
to the effect that he recognised the authority of Armagh, and
had his secretary describe him as *Brianus Imperator Scottorum*
– 'Brian Emperor of the Irish'. That makes quite clear what
Brian's ambition was, and by now he was effectively king
over the whole of Ireland.

About 1012 relationships between Brian and Leinster again
became strained and the dominance which Brian had in general
asserted over Ireland began to provoke a reaction, not only
in Leinster but also in the North. According to later stories,
a personal quarrel instigated by Gormlaith, one of Brian's
former queens, broke out between the king of Leinster and
Brian's son Murchad. As a result the king of Leinster sent
envoys into the north urging the northern rulers to revolt
against Brian. Whatever truth may lie behind the story, the
northern rulers did, in fact, take the field. At the same time
hostilities broke out between Malachy and the Vikings of
Dublin. He ravaged their lands as far as Howth but at Drinan

near Coolock they defeated his forces and killed his son. By the end of 1012, as if expecting major war, Brian fortified north Munster. Late in 1013, possibly in answer to a call for help from Malachy, Brian marched into Ossory and spent almost three whole months ravaging it, and he sent his son Murchad with large forces to attack Leinster. Murchad ravaged Leinster as far as Gendalough, took large booty and appeared at Kilmainham within sight of Dublin. Here he was joined by Brian and together they blockaded the city without success from September to Christmas. Then they broke camp and returned home.

The Leinstermen and their Norse allies knew full well that the attack would be renewed in the early spring of 1014 and they set about building up a confederation of allies to meet this threat. The Vikings of Dublin immediately turned for support to their kinsmen in the Western Isles of Scotland. Sitric, king of Dublin, visited Sigurd, Earl of the Orkneys, who agreed to be in Dublin with his fleet on Palm Sunday 1014. Sitric then went to the Isle of Man where he succeeded in persuading two further Viking leaders, Brodir and Ospach, to support him in the forthcoming struggle. Maol Mórdha, king of Leinster, proved a less successful diplomat and failed to get the support of the south Leinster kings.

Brian, warned of these events, began to muster his forces. However, Connacht held aloof, and only the forces of two small south Connacht kingdoms joined with him. The northern rulers also stood back and took no part whatever in the coming struggle. Ossory, a Munster kingdom, which appears to have fallen more and more into the Leinster sphere of influence, though hostile to Brian, did not participate in the struggle. Apart from Munster and south Connacht, Brian originally had the support of Malachy and the forces of Meath. However, on the eve of the battle a violent dispute arose and Malachy led his troops home. Brian marched to Dublin and sent his son Donnchad to attack Leinster as a diversionary action. Meanwhile, Malachy departed and the Leinster forces made contact with their Norse allies. Battle was joined at Clontarf on Good Friday, 23 April 1014.

It was a long and dogged struggle between almost equally balanced forces and the battle lasted the whole day, which is

very unusual for early Irish battles. Eventually, the
Leinstermen and the Vikings broke rank and were routed with
a great deal of slaughter. Losses on both sides were very heavy.
Brian himself was killed in his tent by Vikings fleeing from
the scene of the battle. His son Murchad and most of the
prominent Munster leaders were slain in the battle and, on
the opposing side Maol Mórdha, king of Leinster, and his
Viking allies, Sigurd and Brodir, were killed. Sitric, king of
Dublin, very wisely kept within the city and survived to tell
the tale. After the battle, Donnchad, Brian's son, led the
battered Munster forces homewards in safety, despite some
opposition from the men of Ossory on the way. Brian's body
was taken to Armagh and was buried with very great
ceremony by the clergy.

The Battle at Clontarf was not a struggle between the Irish
and the Vikings for the sovereignty of Ireland. Neither was
it a great national victory which broke the power of the
Vikings forever. Long before the Battle of Clontarf the
Vikings had become a minor political force in Irish affairs.
Traders and merchants in the cities of Dublin, Wexford,
Waterford, Cork and Limerick, they were no longer of any
military significance in the wars that were being conducted
by the Irish kings. In point of fact, Clontarf was part of the
internal struggle for sovereignty between the great Irish
provincial rulers and it was in essence the revolt of the
Leinstermen against dominance from Munster, a revolt in
which their Viking allies played a very important but
secondary role. Its most important result was not the defeat
of the Vikings but the blow it dealt, in the short term, to the
power of the Munster kings. The subsequent weakness of the
Dál gCais, and indeed of the Uí Néill, gave some chance to
Leinster to revive but within a generation kingship passed
forever from Maol Mórdha and his dynasty, and the grandson
of Brian was later to assert his authority ruthlessly over
Leinster and Dublin.

But in later tradition, both Irish and Viking (there was after
all a thirteenth-century Viking Brian saga), Clontarf became
a heroic battle of saga and storytelling. According to the
stories, fearsome portents and visions were seen by both sides
on the eve of the battle. A fairy woman appeared to Dál gCais

and foretold disaster. Saint Senán appeared to Brian's
followers on the night before the battle, demanding
compensation for Brian's attack on Inis Cathaig, Senán's
monastery, thirty-seven years before, when he killed the king
of Limerick and his two sons. And when Senán was asked to
wait until the morrow, he replied ominously that the morrow
would be too late. In the Isle of Man, where the troops and
ships of Brodir were gathered, there were further fearsome
visions. Brodir and his man saw a rain of blood. The next
night arms fell upon them from the air, and the third night
they were attacked by ravens with iron beaks and claws.
Another Viking saw vision of hell in the form of a river filled
with demons who will drag him down. He saved himself by
promising a pilgrimage to Rome to St Peter saying: 'Your
dog, holy apostle Peter, has twice run to Rome and will run
a third time if you save him.' And evil portents were seen
throughout the Norse world, even in Iceland and Caithness
far away from the scene of the battle.

And so Clontarf became not only an important battle of
history but a great battle of literature. The list of the
combatants was swelled by numerous additions and the
contingents from the Isles and the Isle of Man became the
forces, in time, of the whole Viking world. All the Irish wished
to have one of their ancestors present at the famous battle and
so the list of combatants was swelled in each later telling of
the tale of the battle. Brian himself then became in story what
he never was in fact, the defender of Ireland against the pagan
hordes of Vikings, the saviour of Christianity, the sovereign
ruler of Ireland who led the forces of the nation to victory
over the foreigners. And that, of course, is how he is
remembered in popular tradition.

4. The Norman Invasion of 1169

By Michael Richter

The sense of history is highly developed in Ireland, more so than in any other European country known to me. This series itself is an indication of that phenomenon. A developed sense of history means that people, dates and events of the past are remembered. 1169 is one of those dates, the beginning of the Norman invasion of Ireland. Let us start with a question: since this date is remembered, why then is it not commemorated? Reflecting on this I have come to the conclusion that not all historical dates that are popularly remembered are held worthy to be commemorated. It would be worth investigating why that should be so, why, for example, 1916 is commemorated but not 1169.

The popular view, as I understand it, is that the Norman invasion of Ireland in 1169 was the beginning of about 750 years of a strong if not overwhelming English influence in Ireland's history. This view is not correct, for we shall see that the impact of the Normans was not all that pervasive in the medium term, namely over the subsequent three and a half centuries.

We have to ask how did the Norman invasion come about in the first place, secondly what is known about it, and thirdly how it affected the course of Irish history.

The popular understanding of history is highly personalised, it is that men and women make history. In our case it is the story of Dermot Mac Murrough, how in 1152 he abducted Dervorgilla, wife of Tiernan O'Rourke, and thereby laid the foundation for the hatred that Tiernan bore him; how Tiernan got his chance of revenge in 1166 when he found an ally in Rory O'Connor to stifle Dermot's ambitions; how they exiled him from Ireland, and how Mac Murrough, wishing to regain his kingdom, looked for support in the neighbouring island. Thus the Normans came, or, as more recent scholarship would have it, the Cambro-Normans, that is descendants of Norman nobles who had settled in Wales. Some scholars have gone even further and denied the validity of the term 'invasion' and instead refer to the 'invitation of the Cambro-Normans to come into Ireland'. I still believe that we must speak of an invasion although it was initiated by an invitation. I would like to modify another term: the foreigners who came to Ireland at Mac Murrough's invitation were called 'English' by their contemporaries. I shall thus refer to 'the English invasion of Ireland'.

Such nuances will take a while to be popularly accepted; for the time being, there remains the villain of the piece, Dermot Mac Murrough. In this role he appears to me as the most misunderstood as well as the most over-rated Irishman from medieval times. I maintain that despite what some of his contemporaries wrote about him and the events brought about by him. Thus the continuator of the *Annals of Tigernach* writes under 1170: 'The beginning of Erinn's evil, Robert FitzStephen came into Ireland.' Similarly, the *Annals of the Four Masters*, recording the death of Mac Murrough in 1171, wrote: 'Mac Murrough, king of Leinster, by whom a trembling sod was made of all Ireland.'

If some contemporaries saw the events in that light, how can we question their judgment? Well, I think we can and, indeed, must do just that. We have to take into account that contemporary comments and judgments can be very wrong indeed, mainly because contemporaries lack a medium or long term perspective. We have to take this at least as a working hypothesis. It seems to me that the importance of the English invasion of Ireland in 1169 cannot simply be personalised by shifting the blame onto Mac Murrough. In many ways he did not have the stature to make such an impact. So what is to be done?

To the historians events and dates of the past are largely the tools they work with, not the end product of their efforts. To state that the English invaded Ireland is where we have to start our investigation, not finish it. Of course we must ask how the invasion came about, what was its pre-history. We must say something about the consequences and wider implications of the invasion. But perhaps most important of all, we must investigate the quality of our information about the event, we

must examine those who wrote history as much as those who
– allegedly – made history. Let us first turn to the event itself,
the English invasion of Ireland.

We have to start, not in 1169, but about the year 1155 and
discuss at some length a non-event. About 1155 Pope Adrian
IV, an Englishman, by the way, wrote a letter to the new
English king, Henry II, granting him, on certain conditions,
the right to invade Ireland and reform the Church there. This
document is known as the Bull *Laudabiliter*, after the opening
word of this papal letter. It is important to emphasise that
Laudabiliter was a papal reply to a request sent to Rome in the
name of the English king. The initiative for the idea of
invading Ireland came from England. One can go even further
and specify that the initiative for the request did not lie with
Henry II but with the secretary to the Archbishop of
Canterbury. This was John of Salisbury, later a close associate
of Thomas Becket, and even later bishop of Chartres, the
author of a famous treatise on the ethics of politics called
Policraticus. John acted as agent of Theobald, Archbishop of
Canterbury. He was chosen by the archbishop for this task
because of his close friendship with the pope. Why would
Canterbury push for an invasion of Ireland? This can be fairly
easily explained. The reform of the Irish Church in the first
half of the twelfth century, brought to a rather successful
conclusion at the synod of Kells in 1152, formally severed the
last remaining claims to overlordship of Canterbury over the
Irish Church, the roots of which go back to around the year
600. Such overlordship had never been established in real
terms; but Lanfranc and Anselm of Canterbury had tried to
enforce it in the late eleventh century. Now it was finally
gone, but Canterbury found this hard to accept. Hence the
request for papal permission to invade Ireland in order to gain
control of the Irish Church.

Was the Irish Church in need of reform then? The answer
must be a clear 'no'. It had been reformed between the late
eleventh and mid-twelfth century. It is quite obvious that the
request from Canterbury to Pope Adrian IV was made under
false pretences. But it was granted. However, despite the grant
Henry II did not go to Ireland in 1155 nor for another sixteen
years. And when he went it was in a different function. One

of the reasons why he did not go in 1155 was that the pope had set terms that Henry II had no intention of accepting. For in *Laudabiliter* the pope claimed that Ireland and all other islands that were Christian belonged to the jurisdiction of St Peter. In this subtle way the pope laid claim to jurisdiction over Henry II's main island, England, but the king did not accept this.

So *Laudabiliter* did not initiate an English invasion of Ireland. This is the non-event referred to earlier. It merits discussion here because later generations believed otherwise. In the early fourteenth century it was argued for the first time in Ireland that *Laudabiliter* was instrumental in the English invasion of Ireland. This is demonstrably wrong. We should add, however, that, after the English had established their rule in Ireland, they did gain a large measure of control of the Irish Church. We may add further that from 1213 on the pope had jurisdiction over England and Ireland. Thus in a curious way the main intentions expressed in *Laudabiliter* later came to be realised.

So we turn to the English invasion itself, for such it undoubtedly became despite the fact that the first Anglo-Welsh had been invited by Mac Murrough. This initial invitation gained a momentum that would have been impossible to predict. About the invasion we are exceptionally well informed by a contemporary, Gerald of Wales. What I have said earlier about contemporary writers and their potential unreliability has to be borne in mind with him as well. Gerald of Wales wrote two important books about Ireland, the *Topographia Hibernica* or *Topography of Ireland* and the *Expugnatio Hibernica* or *Conquest of Ireland*. These works are extremely well written and were very widely read, not only in Gerald's lifetime but in the centuries thereafter. Even today a foreigner who wants to get quick and relatively easy information about medieval Ireland is well served by Gerald of Wales. Both works, the *Topography of Ireland* and the *Conquest of Ireland,* have been issued recently in revised translations; they are compulsory reading for anybody interested in the period.

Let it be made quite clear that Gerald of Wales's works about Ireland are not objective history; there is no such thing anyway, and which medieval Irish historian, after all, could lay claim to greater impartiality? To the Irish, Gerald's works are not pleasant to read, for they abound in anti-Irish prejudice. But apart from that they contain so much factual information found nowhere else that no Irish historian of the medieval period can afford to by-pass them. It would be unfair to this period of Irish history as well as to Gerald of Wales to summarise the *Expugnatio Hibernica* in which the first fifteen years of the English invasion are described. Instead, some general remarks about the author may help the reader to appreciate his work better.

Gerald of Wales was of mixed Norman-Welsh descent, grandson of Gerald of Windsor, nephew of Maurice FitzGerald and thus a relative of the Geraldines of Ireland. His *Expugnatio* is primarily a eulogy of the achievements of the Geraldines in Ireland, achievements that he believed were not properly appreciated in England. It is furthermore a work praising the deeds of Henry II in Ireland. Gerald dedicated the *Expugnatio* initially to Henry's son, Richard, Count of Poitou, at a time when it was clear that Richard would soon succeed his father on the English throne. Gerald hoped to gain favour with Richard and subsequent promotion in England. These expectations were not fulfilled, but they help to understand some important aspects of the book.

Gerald wrote the *Expugnatio* between 1185 and 1189, on information largely provided by the participants of the invasion. He wrote them in good Latin as he had learned in long years of studies. The stylistic quality explains in part the permanent appeal of the *Expugnatio* to the reader. Born in Wales in 1146, Gerald had been sent to Paris for study before he was twenty. Paris offered at that time the most advanced level of learning. Gerald had famous teachers there, such as Master Meinerius, who was a pupil of the brilliant and controversial philosopher Peter Abelard, Petrus Cantor and Petrus Comestor, Peter the Eater, as he was called because of his voracious reading. Thus Gerald was taught by some of the people who shaped the European intellectual development of the time, and some of the cosmopolitan, urbane and humanistic atmosphere of Paris was still fresh with him when he wrote his works about Ireland. This had a two-fold effect:

he became a respectable writer by European standards – Petrarch was to praise his style in the fourteenth century; but he also became haughty and condescending towards the Irish whose cultural achievements he failed fully to appreciate.

A general point should be added about the *Expugnatio*. It is very easy to misunderstand it as a record of the advance of the English and Anglo-Welsh in Ireland between 1169 and 1185. While the amount of detail contained in the *Expugnatio* is most valuable, the reader easily over-rates the success of the foreigners in Ireland. For the author wrote to glorify his kinsmen and compatriots; he wrote much about their successes, little about their failures. The series of successes sticks in the mind, and so does the impact of the English king in Ireland. But Gerald could not write a history of the conquest of Ireland in 1189, for such had not happened. By then only a small, albeit important, part of Ireland was controlled by the English, and nobody at the time could know how English control would expand over the next century. It is hard to read the *Expugnatio* without the knowledge of hindsight, but if one does, then the title of the book appears as a bombastic overstatement.

This is not to say that the Anglo-Welsh were not fierce fighters, but they seem to have been forced into the position by some substantial opposition that they encountered from the Irish. In the *Expugnatio* they sometimes appear as desperados who were fighting with the back to the wall and had everything to lose.

It is all the more difficult to read the *Expugnatio* in a balanced way because there is only one other major work by which we can, in parts, check Gerald's account. This is an anonymous poem about Strongbow written in French, known as the 'Song of Dermot and the Earl'. This long poem is biased in favour of the foreigners just as is Gerald's account. From the other side we have the Irish annals as our main source of information. They are disappointing. On the basis of them alone no history of the English invasion can be written. One is tempted to conclude from this that the arrival of the English and Welsh was not all that momentous to the contemporary observers.

We should now look at the English invasion of Ireland, recorded, as it is, mainly in the works of Gerald of Wales, in a wider historical perspective. This has to be done largely on the basis of the Irish annals.

When one looks through the annals for the twelfth century, one is struck by the violence that was in evidence almost every year. Now it is true that medieval annalists – not unlike modern newspaper reporters – record disasters more frequently than normal life, and thus the impression obtained from the annals may well be wrong. We are rarely in the position to put the balance right, but as far as the twelfth century goes, it is surely significant that the Four Masters under the year 1145 have an entry that is almost identical with the one I have quoted on the occasion of Mac Murrough's death: 'Great war in this year, so that Ireland was a trembling sod.'

There is much to be said in favour of the view that Irish history in the twelfth century was indeed more violent than previously. The violence is largely, though not exclusively, connected with the competition for the high-kingship. After the rise of the Munster kings, the first half of the twelfth century is dominated by the phenomenal career of Turloch O'Connor of Connacht, as so well described by Fr Ryan in his O'Donnell Lecture in 1966. This rise implied incessant warfare. Turloch's ambition, like that of the O'Briens before him, was to become king of Ireland. Different from the O'Briens, Turloch employed an amazing amount of naval power. This signalled an important new departure in the evolution of Irish military life.

It is sometimes maintained that the struggle for the kingship of Ireland in the eleventh and twelfth centuries was over Tara; there is little in the sources to justify this view. Tara was by then a symbolic goal at best, and it is rarely mentioned. In practical terms, different from myth and propaganda, the main prize for the contenders to control Ireland seems to have been north Leinster and Meath. Almost inevitably, a very prominent place is thus given in the annals to the kingdom of Dublin. It is normally referred to as the kingdom of the 'foreigner', but these 'foreigners' were very much in demand. Between the battle of Clontarf in 1014 and the English invasion in 1169 there was not one major dynasty in Ireland that did not try hard to get control of Dublin, be it by conquest, or, more frequently, by alliances with the 'foreigners'. In the twelfth century, the most frequent allies of the 'foreigners' of Dublin were the Leinster kings. But even when such an alliance did not exist, any contact with the kingdom of Dublin invariably meant getting involved with Leinster. Its geographical position made that province much more exposed than either Connacht or Munster.

The annals do not tell us why the kingdom of Dublin seems to have become so important in the eleventh and twelfth centuries, but it is undoubtedly a very noticeable change in the Irish political scene. In the past ten years or so we have learned very much that helps us to understand better this importance of Dublin. The archaeological excavations at Wood Quay have shown beyond any doubt how Dublin grew in the eleventh and twelfth centuries to become a very important city, important by European standards. Whereas the annals tell us something about the connections of the 'foreigners' of Dublin with the Western Isles, Scotland and Scandinavia, connections primarily of a dynastic kind, the archaeological excavations have revealed, underneath these dynastic orientations, important trading links of Dublin, links with England, south as well as north, and with the Continent, France in particular.

It has often been remarked that the 'foreigners' of Dublin by the twelfth century were foreigners no longer in a real sense, and the archaeological excavations have endorsed this view. There may well have been much co-operation between the people of the kingdom of Dublin and their neighbours, much intermarriage, and the population even may have been predominantly Irish, but the kingdom tenaciously retained its independence, quite remarkable in view of the impressive enemies like the kings of Munster or Connacht, but more easily understood when the unrivalled strength of Dublin's economic position is remembered.

These are some ideas that may help to put Dermot Mac Murrough and the English invasion into another perspective. Mac Murrough's expulsion from Ireland in 1166 was part of the policy of the new contender for the kingship of Ireland, Rory O'Connor, to gain control of the Dublin region. Mac Murrough's return to Ireland in 1167, his regaining of Leinster, was of little consequence. Things looked very different when the English and Welsh who had followed Mac Murrough's invitation captured Dublin in 1170. They not only captured it, they never lost it. Of course the city by itself was not everything. But just as previous contenders for the kingship of Ireland had aimed at controlling the greater Dublin area, including Kildare and Meath, so did the English. And they held on to that rich area tenaciously, to the very end. It is possible to argue that the holding of this area by the English meant that in future there would be no king of Ireland worthy that name.

Viewed from this angle, the English invasion of 1169 did not change the course of Irish history dramatically. For the greater Dublin area had been outside the reach of major Irish rulers for the previous two centuries; it was to remain so in future.

One may add in parenthesis that the English invasion was only one facet, albeit an important one, of generally growing contacts of Ireland with the European world. Other manifestations of the same phenomenon are visible much earlier. The reform of the Church since the late eleventh century has been mentioned already. In the twelfth century, there arrived the new religious orders of which the Cistercians in particular were internationally orientated. Indeed, the Cistercian Malachy of Armagh, an important figure in the reform of the Church, benefited greatly from his direct contacts with Bernard of Clairvaux, that strong personality who ruled the European Church for decades in fact if not in name.

It is quite obvious that the members of the Irish hierarchy were consciously members of the universal Christian Church first and Irishmen second. Archbishop Laurence of Dublin in particular has come in for criticism because of the way in which he tried to mediate between the natives and the English during the battle over Dublin. It is worth pointing out that all the Irish hierarchy submitted to Henry II in 1172 at the council of Cashel and recognised him as their king.

When we stress that the greater Dublin area merely continued to be outside the reach of major Irish rulers after 1170, one may be tempted to say: '*plus ça change, plus ça reste la même chose'*. But that would be, after all, an over-simplification. This will be apparent when we finally turn to the subsequent developments.

The English were in Ireland from 1169 onwards. It is well known that they never managed to conquer the island completely in the following medieval centuries. For about one hundred years after 1169 their influence expanded until it reached almost four-fifths of Ireland, but then a steady decline set in. One hundred and fifty years after Mac Murrough's 'evil deed', after the defeat of Edward Bruce in 1318, it was apparent to everybody that the English did not dominate Ireland any longer. And in the next two centuries their influence declined further dramatically until it was reduced to the Pale.

What happened under the Tudors and Stuarts will be discussed in the next essay, but it is obvious now that English continuous rule of Ireland did not begin in 1169. What was important for subsequent events was that the English never again lost control of Dublin. Furthermore, unlike the Scandinavian rulers of the eleventh and twelfth centuries, they did not eventually become allies of the Irish.

The English invasion of Ireland in 1169 and the following years is only one stage, though an important one, in a profound re-shaping of Irish history in the post-Viking centuries. The foundation of the city of Dublin by the Norse, dependent as it was on the control of its hinterland, the rich lands of Kildare and Meath, that area that was important in Irish history from the very beginning, opened a new era. Dublin thrived because of the international links established and maintained by the Scandinavian rulers. Their trade connections brought wealth to the city as well as to her kings and made the whole area a prize more and more worth having. The Irish annals are not totally silent on this point. Although they rarely mention traders and merchants, and instead largely concentrate on political and military events, what is apparent from the annals is the growing importance of the kingdom of Dublin in national terms.

In this way, the coming of the English to Ireland changed little enough. Foreigners had controlled Dublin intermittently for a few centuries before 1169. But what control of Dublin implied, and especially in the century before the English arrived, we are only beginning to grasp fully. In this respect, the results of the excavations at Wood Quay may be called a milestone in our understanding of the history of Ireland in the Middle Ages generally.

5. The Flight of the Earls

Margaret Mac Curtain

The Flight of the Earls is one of the unsolved puzzles of Irish history, an episode which the more it yields to investigation, the more it remains an enigma. Why did ninety-nine people led by Ireland's greatest aristocracy sail away from Lough Swilly on a September night in 1607, determined never to return again? How could those men and women in the swiftness of their departure bear to leave wife and child, in one case husband and family, behind? There seemed no obvious cause for flight, no outbreak of persecution, no seizure of lands and houses, no arrests. Moreover the two main characters in the episode were the foremost Gaelic lords of Ulster who had recently made an honourable peace with the monarch of their conquered country and had received back their titles and lands as earls of Tyrconnell and Tyrone.

Despite the puzzling aspects of the Flight of the Earls we know a great deal about the events that led up to it, and from them we can surmise why the decision occurred with such rapidity. More interesting at this point of time we can better understand why the episode assumed such epic proportions in the eyes of contemporaries and how it entered so powerfully the inner consciousness of Ulster's folk-memory. Sometimes an event is significant because it is a symbol, and no symbol is as dramatic as that which signifies farewell. The Flight of the Earls represented a finality of sorts, and like a shock-wave, was absorbed in all its meaningfulness by the society of that time.

Though the departure of the great Hugh O'Neill and his young ally, Rory O'Donnell with their respective retinues appeared like the end of an heroic age, the past it signified had been irretrievably altered by the collapse of the Gaelic forces at the Battle of Kinsale six years earlier. The submission to Queen Elizabeth's deputy, Mountjoy, of Hugh O'Neill at Mellifont two years later and his resumption of his English title and earldom, followed by that of O'Donnell seemed to give a certain sanction to the new order of events. Life had changed for the people of Ulster but stability had been restored. The Nine Years War was over and there was a new monarch, one who had been known to be sympathetic to Ulster in the past when he was king of Scotland. Now he was King James I of Ireland as well as of England, Scotland and Wales and things might be better. They could not be much worse than the final years of the war when famine, disease and despoliation made the countryside desolate, and the cattle scarce. There was then a painful disillusionment about the Flight of the Earls. The ensuing four years of peace had been an illusion. So the Flight became for Gaelic contemporaries a code-word containing the key that unlocked all the emotions and remembered griefs of that epic war and its great heroes, now departed. Together poets and annalists gave the episode a significance which conveyed a reality far in excess of the mere exodus of a group of disgruntled emigrés.

The hurried embarkation at Rathmullen on Lough Swilly for the continent of Hugh O'Neill and his companions took place at the end of the summer. It was well chronicled. In English government circles it was known early in 1607 that Rory, Earl of Tyrconnell, brother of the dead Red Hugh O'Donnell, and his friend Cuconnacht Maguire of Fermanagh wanted to enlist in military service with the King of Spain. Now Hugh O'Neill was not just a restored earl sulking in the aftermath of defeat; he was the reluctant custodian of law and order for the king's deputy in the pacified province of Ulster and he warned O'Donnell to seek permission from King James to transfer to Spain. O'Neill's advice was apparently brushed aside and that summer of 1607 Maguire went to Europe in search of a ship for transport. Suddenly in late August he was back with 'a French ship about the burden of three score tons' which anchored in Lough Swilly. Its captain was John Bath and it stayed nine days near Rathmullen. Immediately Rory O'Donnell was notified and he sent word to Tyrone. Sir John Davies, the Attorney-General, takes up the story. 'The Saturday before the Earl of Tyrone was with my Lord Deputy at Slane. . . he took his leave of the Lord Deputy in a more sad and passionate manner than he used at other times; from thence he went to Mellifont, Sir Garret Moore's house. . . he wept abundantly when he took his leave, giving a solemn farewell to every child and every servant in the house, which made them all marvel, because it was not his manner to use such compliments.'

Evidently O'Neill made his decision to leave rapidly – perhaps too hastily – but he had his reasons. O'Donnell's clandestine departure with the earl's prior knowledge would undoubtedly brand O'Neill as a traitor, and there were other pressing considerations which would make his position intolerable if he remained. Quickly in the following days he mustered his closest relatives and followers. All was accomplished in secrecy. About mid-day on Friday, 4 September old style, on a feast fixed by the Irish annalists as that of Holy Cross, the distinguished company boarded ship and after a delay of several hours fraught with strife and tension, they got away around mid-night. In the words of Tadhg Ó Cianáin whose account is first-hand *'Ba thaithneamhach féithchiúin an oíche, le gaoth aniar aneas.'* They went out to sea on a calm still night with a south-west breeze filling the sails.

Of course, the sudden departure of the Earls and their associates was a heaven-sent opportunity to Lord Deputy Chichester, to Sir John Davies, designers of the Ulster Plantation. But for the relatives left behind, and for the Gaelic population of Ulster, the exodus was the greatest misfortune that had befallen them. Their leaders had flown. The way was now wide open for plantation and re-settlement.

'Pearsa d'uireasa ar chéad is ea a bhí sa long' is how Ó Ciánain, annalist of the Flight, enumerates the ninety-nine who entered the ship. It is our good fortune that Ó Cianain's auto-biographical journal logs that sea-voyage, its tribulations, its happy moments, as well as the main places of their subsequent itinerary in Europe. He ends with their sad scattering, some to Louvain, others to Rome towards the end of 1608. Ó Cianáin himself had to leave his wife behind and his modest farm was sold to give her a little money, perhaps to enable her to join him, we do not know. His journal remains to us, a legacy of his fidelity, not only to the Earl Hugh whom he accompanied but to the learned class to which he belonged.

His account, written in slightly archaic seventeenth century Irish, is lively and informative. There are other sources – which for general purposes we can call the government ones. These are the official records, reports of informers, letters of officials to one another and to the king notifying him of the earls' departure. Beyond the accounts that flowed between Dublin and London, there are other official accounts on the continent, those of ambassadors to their rulers, and of papal nuncios to the Vatican. In all there is an impressive version of the event and the subsequent fate of the passengers. It bore particularly on the sensibility of Catholic European countries and was interpreted as a protest with religious overtones.

But possibly responsibility for casting a kind of dying incandescence over the final years of Ulster autonomy rests with a cluster of fine poets composing in *dán díreach* metre for their own people in Ireland. Eóghan Rua Mac an Bhaird, Fear Flatha Ó Gnímh, Lochlann Ó Dálaigh and many others expressed their grief poetically at the downfall of the O'Donnells and the O'Neills. There is an inexpressible poignancy in Mac an Bhaird's poem about Nuala O'Donnell who forsook her husband, Niall Garbh, when he sided with the English in the Nine Years War and left with her brother Rory in the Flight. *A bhean fuair faill ar an bhfeart,* literally: 'O Woman who found opportunity at the tomb to mourn,' and translated magnificently by James Clarence Mangan as: 'O Woman of the piercing wail'.

Arguably all flight is invariably a diminishment of inner power: conflict is resolved by removing the self from the scene of conflict and in a sense this emotion, a kind of emptiness, is one of the secret pains of exile which the emigré carries like a running sore until time or death removes it. But the Flight of the Earls was more than a decision to opt out. It was a statement. The Gaelic world, enfeebled and mortally laid low, was given a gesture which signified its death. These were the mythic heroes of a medieval world who sailed away from the shore and left our world a mundane place ready for dreary modernisation and bureaucratic centralisation. Heroic ages come to an end; great civilisations *do* collapse and occasionally an episode occurs, a final sad echo to emphasise the finality of its passing. That was how contemporaries felt it. For us with hindsight it was prologue to a new age and we long to hurry along to the next sequence and dismiss it as a regional romance.

But the Nine Years War was not just another Tudor war of conquest. Ulster was the region in the late medieval and Tudor period where the Gaelic way of life was most permanent and entrenched. The Gaelic Lordships of Tyrone, Tyrconnell and Fermanagh, to take the greatest ones, are nowadays difficult for us to comprehend in their cultural complexity of landholding, power and kinship relationships. Simply we recoil from the alien value-system in which they were set and to cross the threshold of that Gaelic world, best done by reading the poetry of that time, is to acknowledge a frame of reference, alien to us, strange and even perhaps distasteful.

The links between the end of one of the most devastating wars between Irish and Tudor conqueror and the Flight of the Earls four years later appear so tangible and apparent that there is a temptation to see one as the cause of the other. Time does not stand still and the years between Mellifont and the embarkation at Rathmullen were ones of adjustment for the two earls to a new role of peace-keeper and even, in the case of Hugh O'Neill, to that of an officer akin to the lord presidentship of Ulster. The peace treaties negotiated separately by O'Neill and O'Donnell were generous in their settlement of landholding, local autonomy and personal entitlement and the new king was prepared to be clement. But if O'Neill and O'Donnell were indulged in their exercise of local power over their followers – the title of 'earl' was one of sole ownership over territory traditionally held by the septs of a Gaelic lordship – they were stripped of their political power. All the apparatus of the new civil administration made its appearance in Ulster and the permanent presence of a substantial government military force was a reminder to both the Earl of Tyrone and that of Tyrconnell of the gradual encroachment of the new order on the old power bases of the lordships. Assizes were convened regularly with all the secular liturgy of sheriffs, justices of the peace, coroners, constables and a network of towns and controlled markets was planned to accompany the new shiring of Ulster as a nine-county project. All of this was quite uncongenial to Hugh O'Neill who by a series of adept negotiations at Mellifont had established ownership over a vast territory, ousting the collateral branches of the O'Neills in the process. Though he was still the supreme challenge to English rule in the province, it was always borne in upon him that the state was crowding in on his exercise of power. Close by James Hamilton, a Scottish coloniser, was busy transforming the lands of Clandeboye, formerly held by Conn O'Neill, one of the great branches of the family, and the ambitious Sir Arthur Chichester made no secret of his desire to be lord president of Ulster and to acquire lands there. O'Neill's catholicism ran deep and the promulgation by royal proclamation against Catholic practices in the heartlands of Dungannon was galling in the extreme to him. The appointment of a cousin of the king, George Montgomery to the sees of Raphoe, Derry and Clogher indicated James's determination not only to anglicise the province but to evangelise it.

For Rory O'Donnell, despite the bait of earldom proffered and accepted in Dublin in 1603, the following years in Tyrconnell witnessed bitter strife between him and his brother-in-law, Niall Garbh. An opportunist to his last breath, Niall had changed sides so often while maintaining constant hostility to the sons of Manus O'Donnell, his wife's brothers, that even Mountjoy admitted that 'Niall Garve would never be made honest'. Unfortunately Mountjoy's successor, George Carew disliked Rory O'Donnell and endeavoured to limit not only the rentals of Rory's new earldom but threw his energies actively into curbing any local autonomy Rory might augment. Unlike Hugh O'Neill, Rory O'Donnell was by no means the undisputed lord of Tyrconnell and the new administration centred in Dublin was vigilant in policing his movements. Meanwhile Niall Garbh remained ceaselessly watchful on his flanks. It was however the presence of an army, the extension of the English judicial system and the energetic pursuit of religious reformation which Rory listed formally as his chief reasons for leaving Ireland. There are still missing clues about why the Flight took place precipitately and why it was initiated by Cuconnacht Maguire of Fermanagh. The Fermanagh lordship was one of the most energetic and developed lordships of the late middle ages and the death of the great lord of Fermanagh in the Nine Years War left it vulnerable to a take-over. Constant and shrewd harassment of two young lords was calculated to try their spirits and teach them acquiescence to their new status. Politically both their positions were far more insecure and untenable than that of O'Neill whose stature in mid-Ulster was formidable. Then was the Flight about loss of status and political power? Yes and no. When an older civilisation is being challenged by a newer self-confident one (which was happening also in the new world to the Incas and the Amerindians with the advance of the Spaniards and the Dutch, French and English) there occurs for the older, defeated civilisation not only a loss of status and political power, but a troubling questioning of identity. Ulster identity suffered a deep shock at this period and was to become confused about its roots, one of which was its Gaelic past. If the Flight of the Earls was a decision to opt out following on a loss of status, this in itself constituted a diminishment of the moral force which went into the Nine Years War.

That is not the same as saying that it brought about the collapse of Gaelic civilisation. That had happened with dramatic suddenness at Kinsale. Some battles lose more than wars: they are milestones, Hastings, Lepanto, Waterloo. For Gaelic Ireland the defeat of Kinsale was the end. What the Flight of the Earls really brought about was the seizure for plantation purposes of the lands of the Gaelic lords who sailed away. Like the wrong move in a game of chess, the Knight could now advance and take the citadel. The long-awaited opportunity impatiently desired by Sir Arthur Chichester could now be implemented. As such, ironically the Flight of the Earls ushered in a new phase of plantation. It facilitated the plantation of Ulster, the most enduring and pervasively colonial of the plantation schemes of the Tudor and Stuart centuries. It enabled the Dublin Administration, a somewhat euphemistic but accurate term for English rule in those centuries, to bring the last independent region of the country under the parliament in Dublin as was evident from the returns of Ulster MPs – all of them planters – in the parliament of 1613. The fact that the earls protested about interference with the practice of their Catholic faith underscored the seriousness of King James's intentions to evangelise in a Protestant form the society of the conquered province. From then on evangelisation was inextricably bound up with settlement patterns in the province of Ulster, a process that had not happened in Munster, or Leix-Offaly in the previous century, and did not effectively take place in the larger Cromwellian Settlement nearly fifty years later.

The sense of loss and dread in those who were left when their lords fled overseas cannot be passed over lightly simply because – as always happens in history – it was the little people who were left behind. Many years later Sir William Petty designer of the Cromwellian settlement remarked that the Irish masses 'had no cause to be grateful to their traditional masters and had benefited from the introduction of English standards', but that kind of rationalising was far from the consciousness of the generation who heard the appalling news of a summer sailing from Lough Swilly on the Feast of Holy Cross, 1607. Victims of legends like the common people in every disaster, their resentment was fanned not against those who left them unprotected but towards the invader who came to demand the spoils of victory. There is always of course a crude sense in which conquest is a modernising force because it releases traditional restraints upon the use of land and gives a freer response to market demands but economic expansion conceals losses for many and perhaps gain for a few. The seventeenth century was to prove that it was not Ireland or Ulster that prospered but those who controlled the country's resources.

We have examined how the Flight of the Earls merits its place in Irish history. Yet if ever a monument were to be erected to that event in Rathmullen it must surely represent the hulk of a ship with purposeful figures crowding around the prow looking outward, not backward. All those who began the Irish diaspora so sorrowfully that September day had no knowledge that they were beginning one of the most splendid pages of Irish history, that of the Irish Abroad.

Europe in the seventeenth century was ready to receive its cargo of Irish nobles. Louvain became a second home and Flaithrí Ó Maolchonaire the Franciscan author of *Desiderius* was the link between the exiles and the Irish Franciscan College of St Anthony which he had founded the previous year. He met the exiles at Douai and accompanied them on the rest of their journey as far as Rome. The Irish Franciscans offered schooling and practical hospitality to the young members of the party and gave back to Irish exiles a sense of belonging and of mission. It is true that the will to live did not burn strongly in that first group of exiles. They were emigrés in the classic sense for whom life's adventure was over. By 1616, the year the great Hugh O'Neill died, he had buried his best-loved son, another Hugh, Baron of Dungannon aged twenty-four years, and the year after his own death, Brian, his youngest boy, died in Louvain, a schoolboy of thirteen.

Rory O'Donnell fared no better. He died in 1608 in Rome and Caffir his brother died that same year. They are all buried in San Pietro in Montorio and to the present day tourists from all over the world with a drop of Irish blood pay their respects to a legendary past by visiting the marble tombs high up in the Gianiculum Hill overlooking Rome. Nor does the melancholy list stop with Rome for Cuconnacht Maguire who had originally secured the ship died in Geneva in 1608. Oh, ill-fated year!

Surprisingly it was the women of the Flight who survived and established traditions of distinction for succeeding generations of Irish in Europe. Living in genteel poverty, left with the task of educating young families and enlisting patronage for them in army careers, their powers of endurance were astonishing. This should not really surprise us. Even a cursory examination of Catherine Magennis, fourth wife of Hugh O'Neill or of Rosa O'Doherty, widow at 18, of Caffir O'Donnell and mother of two children, or of Nuala O'Donnell who had left Niall Garbh and her son Neachtan confirms the presence of male-female complementarity in Gaelic Ulster society. Most visible in the sixteenth century in Iníon Dubh, mother of Red Hugh, Rory and Caffir, is the evidence of women participating in decision making procedures, even councils of war, but also reflected in the resolute minor female characters who either accompanied their menfolk to Europe or remained at home to rear fatherless families and be the recipient of those poignant letters that came irregularly from the continent. One glimpses it in a third generation in the daughter of Rory O'Donnell left behind in Kildare with her mother in 1607, the spirited Mary Stuart O'Donnell who escaped from England to join in 1626 a brother in Flanders whom she had never met. Over the next two centuries wave after wave of Irish families came to Europe winning fame, that Renaissance value, and honour, that Celtic one, in their adopted countries in church, court and military camp.

Ireland it has been said has an unfortunate history but is this partly because we like to dwell on the mournful, the might-have-been? When one looks closely at the Flight of the Earls it comes alive like a marvellous bit of tapestry in which there are dark strands and brightly-coloured ones and in which glow movement and vitality. If I were to pick out one small incident that encapsulates the spirit of that group of self-determined exiles, it is that which was recounted by John Davies. The day was the Wednesday, prior to the Flight:

> On Wednesday night, they say, he travelled all night with his impediments, that is his women and children; and it is likewise reported that the Countess, his wife, being exceedingly weary, slipped down from her horse and weeping said she could go no farther: whereupon the earl drew his sword and swore a great oath that he would kill her in the place, if she would not pass on with him, and put on a more cheerful countenance withal.'

It is the proud enigma which is the Great Hugh O'Neill that constitutes the central mystery of the Flight. Fortunately we possess a portrait of his face, awesome in its power of intelligence and beauty of feature, a lived-in face unified by strength of resolution. This man loved more than any other title that of *The O'Neill*.

6. The Plantations of Ulster

Aidan Clarke

Historians have not greatly concerned themselves with the
connections between Ireland and Scotland, for the good reason
that links, of both physical movement and cultural affinity,
were so close that they have left little recoverable trace. In
important respects, north-east Ireland, north-west Scotland
and their hinterlands were parts of the same ethos. Thus it
was that when the Scottish Highlanders and Islanders were
threatened, in the later sixteenth century, by Protestantism
and by Lowland control, they naturally turned to Ireland as
a place of refuge. And thus it was that the Elizabethan
government, when it took account of its strategic problems,
thought in terms of the north-east of Ireland as an area of high
risk, and contemplated establishing English settlements there
as a buffer against Scottish intrusion.

That perspective was to change with extraordinary
suddenness. When Elizabeth died in 1603, she was succeeded
on the thrones of both England and Ireland by James VI of
Scotland. No political union was involved, but inevitably the
political systems of the king's three separate but contiguous
kingdoms became interlocked, and their problems began to
intertwine. The king's fellow Scots were not slow to profit
from the improvement in his fortunes. Rich and influential
countrymen accompanied him to England, revelling in the
patronage at his disposal. Others, less obtrusively, crossed to
Ireland, settling in significant numbers along the coasts and
valleys of Antrim and Down, where population levels were
low, the land was under-used, and there was room enough
for newcomers without displacing those who were there
already. They came to the same places that Scots had been
coming to for centuries, but they came by new routes from
different places and found an altogether different welcome.
These were Lowland Protestants rather than Highland
Catholics, welcome allies of the state, not unruly intruders,

and they represented a wholly new departure in the tradition of Scottish relations with Ireland. Their migration was voluntary and unstructured, a response to economic opportunities rather than government inducements, but there were, of course, leaders and followers, and the process was not disorderly: estates were created, villages constructed, towns planned, and a modest prosperity achieved on the basis of Scottish markets. Though some local landholders were tricked or forced out of their possessions, others saw the advantage of letting some of their land to wealth-producing tenants, and encouraged the movement.

Though this settlement was not displeasing to the government, it was far from conforming to the rigorous principles of colonisation as they had evolved through the sixteenth century. What contemporaries called 'plantation' was by now a sophisticated concept. When first used, the term had merely expressed the crude belief that if the Irish could be replaced by imported English, all would be well. Before long, in Leix and Offaly, it was translated into a severely practical plan to protect the Pale against the midland Irish by introducing a militarised settlement on its weakest frontier. This idea of plantation, as a way of stabilising trouble-spots or providing a reliable defensive screen in vulnerable areas, like south-west Munster and east Ulster, survived. But it was overlaid by the notion that plantation might be a ready means of contributing to what had become the ulterior goal – the anglicising, or civilising, of Ireland. The implications were worked out in detail when a part of Munster, perhaps eight per cent of the province, was planted in the 1580s at a time when plans to promote settlement in the new world across the Atlantic had inspired a good deal of constructive thought about what colony building actually entailed. Three basic principles were established for Munster: first, that the settler communities should faithfully recreate the structure of rural England, a numerical model of which was devised, specifying the exact mix of freeholders, copyholders, leaseholders, cottiers, artisans and others required to achieve the ideal social profile on each estate; second, that these communities should be absolutely segregated from all contact with the natives; and third, that settlers should be Protestants of English birth. The intention was not merely to establish areas of control and support, but to provide a model of civilised practice which would persuade by its manifest superiority, and leaven the Irish mass by the example of its success.

The Munster experiment did not succeed, not least because it proved impossible to put the principles into effect, but the ideas remained, and when, some twenty years later, the flight of the earls allowed the government to re-think its Ulster policy, a plantation scheme, modified by experience, was one of the obvious options. The circumstances made both aspects of the plantation tradition relevant: on the one hand, the sinister departure of O'Neill and O'Donnell and the subsequent rebellion of O'Doherty in Inishowen seemed to show that the pacification of Ulster had not succeeded; on the other, anglicisation was still the government's goal, and the opportunity to make quick progress by importing it ready-made into the heartland of Gaelic civilisation was difficult to resist.

There were, moreover, national considerations as well as regional ones. When the Tudor military conquest ended at Mellifont, and the government took control of all Ireland for the first time, unexpected political difficulties emerged. Foremost among them was the presence of different and competing colonial communities in Ireland. The Elizabethan settlers had been the partners of the state in the conquest, they were attuned to contemporary English values and attitudes, and they enjoyed the government's favour. The descendants of those who had preceded them to Ireland, in some cases by more than four hundred years, had failed to adjust to fundamental changes which had taken place in their mother country. Though they prided themselves on their ancestry, proclaimed their loyalty to the government and supported its anglicising policies, they had remained Catholic when England became Protestant. Their loyalty was to an England which no longer existed, and it was unwelcome. The government had taken it for granted that English victory in the Nine Years War was, by definition, a victory for Protestantism. It was taken aback to find that an English heritage of legal and constitutional restraints upon government action enabled the Catholic colonial community to resist policies which threatened its interests. One of the attractions of planting Ulster was the possibility of altering this unsatisfactory balance of local power by establishing a new colony to act as a counterweight to the old one.

Thus, plantation in Ulster was not intended merely as a means of suppressing the Ulster Irish: it was also a way of overcoming the influence of the community of Catholic colonists. This frank recognition that conquest and control must ultimately involve disowning the pre-reformation settlers set the scene for the dominant theme of seventeenth century Irish history – the expropriation and degradation of the Catholic colonists, which was accomplished by the Cromwellian and Williamite confiscations, and consolidated by the penal laws.

The final element in the situation was the king himself. James was a munificent monarch, though mean with cash in hand, and he understood very well the politics of patronage. He had found the English crown less well endowed than he had expected, and Ulster presented him with the opportunity to repay obligations, confer favours and indulge his taste for grand regal gestures. When it became clear, in 1608, that almost all of the six counties of Armagh, Cavan, Derry, Donegal, Fermanagh and Tyrone were at his disposal, he found himself in the enviable position of being able to forward his Irish policies by sharing out the spoils of Elizabeth's victory. It was spoilsmanship that dictated that there should be four categories of beneficiary – the English, the Scots, the Protestants in Ireland, and the Irish. The English and Scots were at the heart of the scheme that evolved: one hundred undertakers, half of them English and half Scots, received grants amounting in all to about one-quarter of the available land on low-rent development contracts that bound them to import specified numbers of settlers in defined categories, and prohibited them from having anything to do with the native Irish. Fifty 'servitors' – army men who had remained in Ireland after serving in command positions during the Nine Years War – were now rewarded with grants totalling about one-fifth of the confiscated territory, and encouraged, though not compelled, to replace the Irish with imported settlers. Somewhere between one-fifth and one-quarter of the area was granted to three hundred natives, deemed to be 'deserving Irish', who were chosen partly in recognition of co-operation in the past, but partly to ensure that there was a vested Irish interest in the new arrangements, however unsatisfactory. The remaining land was set aside to endow the church and support education, or frittered away in special grants of one kind or another. One entire county, however, the county of Derry, was left out of the general scheme and handed over to the City of London to manage. To some extent, this was because the intended development of Derry and Coleraine as commercial centres needed special capabilities, but it was also a bid to secure prestige and capital for the project, which was less eagerly supported in England than it was in Scotland.

The scheme transformed Ulster, and indeed Ireland – but not according to plan. Though Ulster historians have written lyrically of the sturdy, hard-working, self-disciplined virtues of their ancestors, it is clear enough that Ulster, like other colonies, attracted its share of opportunists, misfits and refugees from justice. It is equally clear, from the evidence of trade, which continued to be predominantly in pastoral and natural products, that the economic activity of the region was not dramatically transformed by the plantation. There was a quickening, and an increasing commercialisation, but the aim of replacing Gaelic pastoralism by a more civilised arable economy was not quickly achieved: livestock production was too profitable and too well suited to the conditions to be renounced as fit only for a primitive society.

Social life changed, of course. Some four thousand families came to the plantation counties in the first fifteen years, and perhaps half as many had made their homes in Antrim and Down. Manor houses and bawns, towns and villages with their churches and mills, altered the physical face of the province. Fixed boundaries and new property laws constrained the Irish, many of whom chose exile. Those who did not were hemmed in by fences and leases where they had formerly moved freely with their cattle. But segregation came slowly, pragmatically and patchily. The official plan was undermined from the beginning by incompetent measurement and opportunism. All the undertakers received far more land than they had contracted for, and they soon discovered that they could place the stipulated number of settlers on the land, and still have plenty left over. Arguably, that fact made the plantation possible, for the undertakers were underfinanced and almost all of them quickly learned to generate their working capital by leasing land to the Irish. So, in the first phase, settlers and natives lived side by side. But the distribution of settlement had been based on political rather than economic geography, and a slow sorting-out process soon commenced. As the early settlers learned of better land, better terms or better markets in some other part of the province, they moved: and new settlers, coming speculatively rather than by arrangement, were guided by the same considerations. It was in this second phase that the prime settlement areas were identified, and the Irish forced on to the inferior lands. By the same process, the original arrangement which had kept the Scots and English settlers apart from one another broke down. As they intermingled, the influence of the more numerous and more homogeneous Scots came to predominate. Meanwhile, the 'deserving Irish', who carried a disproportionate responsibility for their people, and who found it difficult to think in commercial terms and to charge economic rents, fell into debt, sold off their lands, and declined in numbers and importance. In short, there were few respects in which the developing plantation conformed to the intentions of those who planned it, and the only obvious difference between the government's official plantation and the uncontrolled and unplanned settlement of Antrim and Down was that Antrim and Down were more densely settled.

Even the political benefits proved illusory. In the short term, the plantation did yield quick dividends. At a parliament convened in 1613, members were returned from newly created Ulster constituencies in sufficient numbers to outvote the representatives of the Catholic colony: the government seemed justified in looking forward to taking full control of Irish political institutions and depriving the Catholic colonists of their constitutional defences. The outcome was less simple.

It had been naïve, perhaps even disingenuous, to introduce Scots to Ulster as agents of anglicisation – for they were not themselves anglicised, and they did not become so. Though they acknowledged the authority of the Dublin government, they never related closely to the capital nor to the administration. It was to Scotland that they sent their children to be educated: it was from Scotland that they drew their ministers of religion. Their trade was with Scotland, and so were their sympathies and interests. So close was the connection that for a time some of them travelled to Scotland and back on Sundays for religious service. People like these could be relied on to support the English administration in Dublin only so long as relations between England and Scotland remained friendly. In the 1630s, in the reign of James's son, Charles I, this condition ceased to exist. Partly because Charles appeared to regard Scotland as an English dependency rather than as an independent kingdom, partly because he tried to reform the Church of Scotland along English lines, Scottish hostility mounted, war became imminent, and the Lord Deputy of Ireland seriously envisaged the possibility of sending the Scots in Ulster back to Scotland. They had become, he believed, a greater threat to the established order than the Irish themselves. When an Irish parliament convened in 1640, he found himself in the ironic position of having to rely upon the support of the Catholic colonists to outvote the members from Ulster.

On both sides of the Irish Sea, religion was at the root of the problem. Though there were bishops in the Church of Scotland, the Scottish church was, in essentials, Presbyterian. In theology, liturgy and organisational principles it differed sharply from the Church of England. It differed less from the Church of Ireland, which was small, exclusive and evangelically unsuccessful; quite capable of servicing the small number of Protestants in Ireland at the beginning of the seventeenth century, but unable to respond effectively to the massive injection of Protestants into Ulster, where it had never had a foothold. It welcomed the newcomers, and brought them formally into its organisational framework without inquiring too closely into their orthodoxy. For their part, they went their own way, and behaved as if they were a branch of the Church of Scotland. In this, the Church of Ireland was not being unprincipled: at the time of the plantation, its own liturgical and theological preferences were to the left of the English church. But under new and stronger leadership in the

1630s, the Church of Ireland altered its Articles of Belief, demanded genuine conformity, and deliberately challenged the individuality of the religion of the Scots in Ulster, just as Charles did in Scotland itself.

Events were to postpone the resolution of this conflict within Irish Protestantism for more than twenty years. In 1640, Scotland defeated England in a brief war: in 1641, rebellion broke out in Ireland, and in the following year civil war began in England. When the turmoil in the three kingdoms finally ended with the restoration of Charles I's son, Charles II, in 1660, a new religious settlement was devised in Ireland which recognised the existence of Presbyterianism while assigning an inferior status to its subscribers. Thenceforward, in a province in which not a single acre of land remained in Catholic ownership, colonial society was divided between a privileged minority of established church members, largely English in origin, and a majority of Scottish Presbyterians who suffered both religious and civil disabilities.

The rebellion of 1641 was not originally an attempt to overthrow the plantation of Ulster, though it became one. It was planned by the 'deserving Irish', not by the dispossessed, and its timing and objectives were dictated by events in England and Scotland rather than in Ireland. But those who planned it, with limited political aims in mind, soon lost control of it: the dispossessed unleashed their resentments, atrocities were committed, and returned exiles sought to turn the movement into a war to procure the redress of their historic wrongs. The plantation, however, was not overthrown. Throughout the 1640s, a Scottish army was stationed in Ulster to defend the emigrant brethren, and though it is chiefly remembered for its defeat by O'Neill at Benburb it served its purpose. The colony, weakened by massacre, war, famine, plague and flight, nonetheless survived and began to rebuild itself during the Cromwellian 1650s when inward migration once more resumed. In the outcome, the settlements were more secure, and even more Scottish, after the rebellion than before it. The control of the Dublin government was surer, but Ulster remained ambivalent, becoming reluctantly more integrated into Ireland, but continuing to be no less closely bound up with Scotland.

King James I was angrily disillusioned with the way in which his plantation developed. A commission of inquiry reporting in 1622 confirmed his judgment and deemed the plantation a failure. By the relevant terms of reference, which were those of the original scheme, the king and his commissioners were right: the scheme did fail. But its effect was to free the way for the migrationary flow that had already spilled into Antrim and Down to spread across the north of Ireland, where it produced an organic society more complex, vigorous and resilient than the artificial model that it swept aside in the process. That was not the work of a single generation. Just as the inward movement of Highland Scots had been going on long before the plantation, so the movement of the Lowlanders and Borderers continued long after it. The settlement of the plantation period provided a thrust which was not sustained from within but from the steady traffic that reinforced it with fresh settlers from Scotland throughout the century.

That process of organic evolution and renewal set these settlements apart from the plantation projects which were undertaken in other parts of Ireland, each of which, like Ulster, was designed to be self-sustaining – to grow from its own resources, as the image of plantation implies – but none of which proved viable. The plantation ideal recognised that self-contained, segregated communities must be composed of the right mixture of people of all social roles and economic functions: plantation administrators found that ideal impossible to achieve. Outside Ulster, those settlers who did not arrive as landholders, freeholders or substantial tenants either quickly achieved that status or gradually crossed the cultural divide and were lost to memory among the natives. The twin processes, of the aggrandisement of settlers and the expropriation of native and colonial Catholic landholders, left the settlers as a privileged and propertied minority, separated from the rest of the population by social class and economic circumstances, as well as by religion – so that their ascendancy, though it had a religious character, was most significantly expressed in their ownership of the means of production. Within Ulster, the position was otherwise. There, the settler community was genuinely composed of all social and economic classes. Though discrimination certainly prompted some Presbyterians of property to seek social acceptance by conforming to the established church, it impelled most of them to a fierce affirmation of their distinctiveness. At the lower end of the social scale, religion and ethnic affinity became proud badges of settler superiority over natives from whom they actually differed little in material circumstances.

The nature of the religion which distinguished these settlers, not only from the Irish but from the English fellow-colonists whose privileges they disputed, was enormously important in moulding their collective character. Their central belief was in predestination: that is to say that they held that the ultimate destiny of every human being was determined by God before birth, and was unaffected by human endeavour. Some were chosen for salvation, and these were the elect; the remainder were doomed to damnation. It was a harsh and implacable doctrine, and it imparted an attitude of mind that accorded well with the ideology of colonialism, and perhaps particularly well with the psychological needs of lower class colonists who, though they could not aspire to belong to the social elite, might claim the higher status of membership of the elect of God. The Pope they regarded as Anti-christ, Catholicism as a Satanic conspiracy against the truth, and their Irish neighbours as its unregenerate agents. It was a comforting perspective. At one level, it justified the injustice inherent in colonialism: at another, it was an inexhaustible source of pride and confidence. It was embraced with an impassioned intensity of conviction which transcended social differences and welded the community of believers into a coherent and integrated force – and which, in important respects, has transcended time, change and modernisation.

7. The Act of Union

James McGuire

How did they pass the Union?
By perjury and fraud;
By slaves who sold their land for gold
As Judas sold his God.
By all the savage acts that yet
Have followed England's track,
The pitch-cap and the bayonet,
The gibbet and the rack;
And thus was passed the Union
By Pitt and Castlereagh;
Could Satan send for such an end
More worthy tools than they?

These lines of poetry are attributed to John O'Hagan, a Newry born lawyer and a high court judge from 1881. They do not constitute great poetry but they do typify nineteenth and twentieth century nationalist and liberal attitudes towards the Union. All the ingredients are there, explicitly or implicitly: the union as a betrayal of Ireland, an English plot, approved not only by traitors but corrupt traitors at that, and all at the behest of an English government prepared both to bribe the legislators and to provoke and terrorise the countryside.

The poem was quoted approvingly by the nationalist MP, J. G. Swift MacNeill, in his *Constitutional and Parliamentary History of Ireland* as 'indicating the passionate resentment with which the Irish race at home and abroad regard this stupendous crime'. James Carty subsequently included a brief quotation from the judge's poem in his *Junior History of Ireland*, a much more influential work than Swift McNeill's, since it formed the historical opinion of generations of Irish school children. Carty's own comment on the passing of the Union was almost as poetic as the judge's verse:

Patriots spurned Castlereagh's bribes,
but ignoble men agreed to sell their country,
and so the Union was passed.[1]

One could give many more instances from political tract or history text of similar attitudes to the act of union. Even Gladstone referred to it in 1886 as 'the blackest and foulest transaction in the history of man', a description which suggests a certain proneness to exaggeration on his part.[2]

What was this act of union which produced such rhetorical flourishes from the learned and the great? There were in fact two acts of union, one passed by the Irish parliament in College Green, the other by the parliament at Westminster. It was the Irish act which produced the anger and resentment and with which I am concerned. (The British act made the necessary legal and constitutional arrangements consequent on the passing of the Irish act.)

As a result of these acts of union the kingdom of Ireland was merged with the kingdom of Great Britain (itself an amalgam since 1707 of the kingdoms of England and Scotland) into a newly constituted United Kingdom of Great Britain and Ireland. The Irish parliament was abolished and provision was made for Irish representation in the new union parliament at Westminster. Although some of the trappings of the kingdom of Ireland survived the union (the viceroy, the Irish privy council, the separate Irish judiciary), its main effect was to create a single constitutional entity with the body politic of both islands represented in the same legislature at Westminster.

While the origins of the Irish parliament, which the union abolished, went back to the thirteenth century and while its internal development was closely parallel to its English counterpart, it had a more chequered history. For much of the period after the Reformation it was regarded by government as an occasional expedient, summoned to vote supplies, make religious changes or legalise plantations. All this changed, however, in the eighteenth century as government finances required frequent recourse to parliament for supply. In this way the Irish parliament became an indispensable part of governmental and political life in the last century of its five hundred year lifespan.

How representative was the eighteenth century Irish parliament? An analysis of its membership shows that it was overwhelmingly landed gentry in composition, though lawyers (who were usually members of gentry families) and some merchants were elected to the Commons. The rising middle class manufacturers and traders were effectively excluded from parliament, as were all Roman Catholics, even surviving members of the landed gentry. In all these characteristics it resembled its British counterpart. The electorate which returned members to sit in the Commons was also strictly limited since the vote was based on property qualifications. (From 1727 Catholics were excluded from voting, even if otherwise qualified.) However, even this narrowly-based electorate only really functioned in a small number of open constituencies, the counties and large towns. The vast majority of the remaining constituencies had only nominal electorates and were usually under the control of borough patrons, indeed they were regarded as the personal property of the patron (and patrons were quite prepared to sell their 'property' if circumstances required it and the price was right).[3]

How limited or how considerable were the powers of the eighteenth century Irish parliament? For most practical purposes it enjoyed political and legislative powers similar to those of the Westminster parliament in Great Britain. The same sort of concerns dominate the journals and statutes of both parliaments. But there were a number of areas in which the Irish parliament's significance was considerably less important. In the first place the Dublin administration was not responsible to the Irish parliament in the same way that the king's ministers were becoming increasingly answerable to Westminster; secondly, Whitehall maintained a veto on Irish legislation through the convoluted operations of Poynings' law; thirdly, the Westminster parliament up to 1782 could pass legislation binding Ireland over the heads of the Irish parliament when English or imperial interests were at stake (though it must be added that this legislative supremacy was exercised with comparative infrequency).

These constitutional restrictions or inhibitions caused

periodic resentment in eighteenth century Ireland, but it was the impact of American developments in the 1770s which turned this occasional anger into a consistent and eventually successful demand for the Irish parliament's legislative independence. At first the outbreak in 1776 of the American War of Independence found Protestant Ireland anxious and determined to preserve domestic order and to secure the country from external enemies, a very real danger when France and Spain joined in on the side of the American colonists. These were the circumstances in which the Volunteers were founded to act as an unofficial militia and at a time when much of the regular army had been withdrawn for service in America. But if the Volunteers' initial purpose was to defend king and country from internal and external threats, the growth in resentment at British interference with Irish trade at a time of economic slump found a ready-made outlet in meetings of Volunteer companies. Despite British commercial concessions in 1779, it was not long before the constitutional problem, the British parliament's power to legislate for Ireland, became the focal point for complaint. This growing politicisation of the Volunteers was paralleled by the emergence of an effective and highly articulate 'patriot' (their own term) opposition in the Irish parliament.

While the British government became increasingly alarmed at the forcefulness of Volunteer demands and the support they were receiving from within the College Green parliament, it is quite arguable that legislative independence need not have been conceded since Protestant Ireland was hardly likely to emulate the American revolutionaries. However, the collapse of the British government under Lord North in the wake of military disaster in America had a dramatic result. The new Whitehall administration quickly conceded the Irish claims and the necessary legislation was passed by the Westminster parliament. Legislative independence had been achieved.

This achievement has always been associated with Henry Grattan, the MP for Charlemont and the emancipated parliament of 1782 is usually remembered, quite misleadingly, as Grattan's parliament. In fact it remained, despite Grattan's reforming efforts, the same unreformed and unrepresentative assembly, even in terms of Protestant Ireland, that it had been before 1782. Yet Grattan was its orator and it was his rhetoric which greeted legislative independence in 1782:

> Spirit of Swift, spirit of Molyneux,
> Your genius has prevailed.
> Ireland is now a nation.[4]

But if this was Grattan's most quoted speech, it was not his most dramatic intervention in the Irish House of Commons. That occurred eighteen years later, in 1800, when an ailing Grattan returned to sit in a House of Commons whose demise seemed inevitable. Once again his rhetoric thrilled his fellow MPs, but it did not alter their votes; and so, only eighteen years after the triumph of 1782, the Irish parliament voted itself out of existence. What had gone wrong? Why was legislative independence so short lived? How was it terminated?

It was not until early June 1798 that the British prime minister, William Pitt, and his government decided to make a legislative union of Britain and Ireland a matter of immediate government policy. They did so for two reasons. First, there were the alarming reports from Ireland that insurrection had broken out in several counties and this despite earlier confident predictions from Dublin Castle that the sitiuation was well under control. Secondly, and potentially more serious, were the intelligence reports from France that Bonaparte had sailed from Toulon with a large fleet. In fact this turned out to be the start of his Egyptian campaign but in London it was feared that the French were bound for Ireland. Faced with internal rebellions and external threats, it was crucial to give the Irish situation immediate attention once and for all. Reinforcements were dispatched to Ireland to deal with the military crisis and Pitt and his ministers drew up plans to solve the Irish problem.[5]

Of course this decision to make union a matter of government policy was not arrived at out of the blue in the summer of 1798. The possibility of union had been discussed at Whitehall during April and May and Pitt himself had long before reached the conclusion that it would be a far better way of governing Ireland than the arrangements which had obtained since the granting of legislative independence in 1782. Even before the French revolution had begun to change the face of British and European politics, the 1782 Anglo-Irish arrangement seemed to Pitt to be fraught with administrative uncertainty and potential dangers. In 1782 no constitutional definition had been given to the relationship of the two kingdoms and when an attempt was made in this direction with the Commercial Propositions in 1784, it had been spurned.

More serious still was the regency crisis of 1788-89 when the Irish parliament seemed to be insisting on its right to decide the terms on which a regent would be appointed for the kingdom of Ireland during George III's incapacity, regardless of whatever was decided in Great Britain. Only the king's recovery to health abruptly ended that crisis, but the problem could arise again. By the end of the 1780s, therefore, to Pitt and a few others union already looked like a desirable solution.

But the crises of the 1780s were as nothing compared with the impact of events in France on Irish politics and opinion from 1789 onwards. Liberally inclined politicians, who had unsuccessfully tried to reform the Irish parliament after legislative independence, together with their extra-parliamentary sympathisers, Volunteer reformers, middle-class business and professional men, were now stimulated by French principles of liberty, equality and fraternity and by the example of what was actually happening within France (at least in the early days of the revolution). In this respect Irish reformers and radicals were no different from their counterparts in Britain and throughout Europe, who saw in French developments hope for their own political emancipation. But in Ireland there was an additional complication, religion. The Roman Catholic middle classes were also becoming increasingly politicised and determined to press for emancipation. How could they be excluded from the benefits of reform? Yet reform of the Irish parliament and political emancipation for Catholics would mean, sooner or later, a Catholic majority in the Commons, a prospect which horrified conservatively inclined MPs and the Protestant landowners whom they represented, and caused even liberal Protestants some anxiety.

The prime minister, William Pitt, was anxious to separate Catholic aspirations from the increasingly radical programme of the newly formed United Irishmen; Catholicism as a religion was after all a force for conservatism and stability. So he suggested, tentatively, linking Catholic emancipation with union. The former would satisfy moderate Catholic demands for relief: 'The Protestant interest in point of power, property and church establishment would be secure because the decided majority of the supreme legislature (i.e. a union parliament at Westminster) would necessarily be Protestant.'

Pitt made this suggestion in 1792 but he did not persist when it received a cool response from the then viceroy in Dublin.[6] Instead he more or less forced the Dublin administration to get a modest Catholic Relief Act passed by the Irish parliament, a measure which restored the vote, but not of course the right to sit in parliament, to some Roman Catholics on the basis of a property qualification.

Pitt's experience of the ascendancy's intransigent opposition to Catholic relief in the early 1790s coloured his attitude towards them and convinced him that their exclusive political dominance in Ireland should be moderated by a union of the two kingdoms.

Of course it must be mentioned that there were too some hardline members of the ascendancy who were coming to the conclusion that ultimately their future security lay in a united kingdom in which Irish Catholics would be a minority in the body politic. But this view was not shared by many in the early 1790s and it took the 1798 uprising for a larger number among the ascendancy to question the durability of their political and social hegemony in a separate kingdom.

Meanwhile events in the Irish countryside were equally disturbing to government and gentry. Since mid-century there had been periodic bouts of agrarian unrest, particularly in Munster and Ulster, and by the 1790s these had taken on markedly sectarian overtones, with Catholic and Protestant peasants fighting over a diminishing stock of available land as the population continued to expand rapidly.[7] Indeed the 1790s and not the 1690s mark the beginnings of the sectarian polarisation of Irish society with the emergence of Catholic Defenders and Protestant Orangemen. Into this cauldron of peasant rivalry and discontent the United Irishmen introduced political and social radicalism, thus adding a degree of Jacobin rhetoric to an already tense countryside.

The threat which the politicisation of the peasantry was perceived as posing to the landed classes can be gauged by the ferocity with which United Irish and Defender activities were crushed in the mid 1790s. This lack of rapport between Protestant landowner and Catholic peasant, indeed the total lack of social cohesion in certain parts of the country, indicated still further to English eyes that the eighteenth century experiment of leaving Ireland to the Anglo-Irish had not worked. Pitt's doubts about the ascendancy' attitudes and methods and his anxiety to distance the London government from them is epitomised in his warning to the viceroy in 1798 to 'resist with as much firmness the intemperance of your friends as the desperate efforts of the enemy'.[8]

Pitt was not obsessed with Irish affairs; far from it, indeed. As Lord Camden remarked to him in 1796: 'I believe as you candidly acknowledged to me before I came hither that Ireland occupies little of your thoughts.'

Yet whenever Ireland surfaced on Pitt's horizon it seemed that its constitution, its politics and society itself were falling apart. But it took the combination of external threat and internal insurrection in May 1798 to galvanise Pitt and his ministers into action; as John Beresford wrote a few months later, in words that could be an epitaph for so much of British government attitudes towards Ireland long before and long after 1798:

> I am very happy that Mr Pitt is thinking on the subject of Ireland, the great misfortune of which country has been that for many years ministers have never thought of her, except when she became extremely troublesome to them, when by some temporary expedient, they have patched up a temporary quiet and left things to chance until another crisis called upon them to think again.[9]

In 1798 Pitt and his ministers were certainly thinking again. Having decided on a union the problem now was to get it through the Irish parliament.

It took two years and two parliamentary bills to get the union on to the Irish statute book. The first bill was presented to parliament in 1799 but was defeated by a coalition of MPs

opposed to union for two quite separate reasons. The
following January a union bill was again presented and by the
early summer of 1800 it had gone through all stages with
comfortable majorities. What had happened in the intervening
months to get parliament, in particular the House of
Commons, to change its mind? As we saw at the beginning,
traditional interpretations stressed almost exclusively the rôle
of corruption, and this view was shared by both nationalist
and unionist writers throughout the nineteenth century: MPs
had their price and sold their consciences for large government
pensions. And there is no doubt that, even by the standards
of the late eighteenth century, the persuasive techniques
adopted by government parliamentary managers and accepted
by some MPs were quite unseemly. The contemporary
comments of the viceroy, Lord Cornwallis, convey a genuine
repugnance at what was expected of him:

> My occupation is now of the most unpleasant nature, negotiating
> and jobbing with the most corrupt people under heaven. I despise
> and hate myself every hour for engaging in such dirty work, and
> am supported only by the reflection that without a union the
> British empire must be dissolved.[10]

Similarly the comments of the chief secretary, Lord
Castlereagh, indicate the sort of preparations deemed
necessary to see the measure through:

> You can easily imagine the complicated negotiations of private
> objects we are at present incessantly engaged in. Every individual
> is now playing his game as if it was his last stake, and it is most
> difficult to meet their expectations, in any degree within the
> possibility of accomplishment.[11]

But is it enough to stress corruption as the explanation for
the passing of the union? Surely some members who
supported it in 1799 and again in 1800 did so out of fear at the
events of 1798? And was there not a built-in disadvantage on
the opposition side in that they were two very disparate
groups, opposing union for quite different reasons: on the one
hand those, like Henry Grattan, to whom union meant the
end of the 1782 achievement and the liberal ambition that some
day the Irish parliament might be both reformed and open to

propertied Catholics; on the other hand those like John Foster, the speaker of the Commons, who feared that union would soon be followed by Catholic emancipation (as Pitt indeed was promising the Catholic bishops and prominent laymen) and that once Catholics were admitted to a full share in public life they would start campaigning for repeal of the union, thus threatening the Protestant ascendancy. So while the Fosters and the Grattans could co-operate in opposing the union, they normally could not agree on any constitutional alternative which would provide Ireland with political and social stability.

But disunity of purpose among the opponents of union does not in itself explain how the government achieved a majority in 1800. After all they had been defeated on the issue just twelve months earlier. In explaining this change in the government's fortunes, historians nowadays point to the fact that few of those who voted against the union in 1799 changed sides in 1800 – in other words they did not sell their consciences. Those who were persuaded to vote for union in 1800 through offers of place and pension were either neutral in 1799 or had subsequently come into the Commons through by-elections and the co-operation, bought at a price, of borough patrons. And the same was true of the anti-unionist side. Even Henry Grattan, who had retired from politics in 1797, was able to make his dramatic return to oppose the union through the timely purchase of a seat.[12]

Another consideration which earlier historians and propagandists ignored was the role of public opinion in late eighteenth century politics. In open constituencies MPs could not ignore the views of the enfranchised and articulate. Two examples will suffice. Dublin MPs voted against the union, reflecting the considerable concern in the capital at the likely loss of commerce and a general decline in Dublin's importance in the event of a union. Cork MPs, however, voted for union since opinion in Cork believed that the city would benefit commercially.[13] In showing due regard for the views of his constituents an MP in an open constituency was being no more than realistic should he wish to continue his political career at Westminster after the union.

What were the consequences for Ireland of the act of union? The traditional view is well expresses by James Carty:

The supporters of the union claimed that it would bring Ireland great benefits. These claims were not fulfilled. In spite of the promises made to them, the Catholics were not emancipated. Protestants still held all the important positions. . . Ireland's trade and industry decayed. The people were worse off than ever.[14]

This was the sort of interpretation argued by George O'Brien, the economic historian of the early twentieth century. But the equation of legislative independence with prosperity and union with economic decline finds little support in the work of modern economic historians.[15] It is now generally accepted that the union had little impact on the economy one way or the other, with the possible exception of fiscal arrangements. The population was already expanding rapidly before the union and it continued to do so afterwards and with far more significant results for the economy and society than any legislative measure. The economic boom created by the European war continued until 1815, both the volume and value of Irish exports increasing rapidly and causing a consequential rise in prosperity for some sections of the community. Meanwhile the poor and deprived continued to be poor and deprived. When the slump in prices and decline in prosperity hit Ireland in the second decade of the nineteenth century it was caused by the impact of peace time conditions on an economy adjusted to wartime expansion.

For many of the Anglo-Irish ascendancy the union meant an end to their political careers. In place of 300 seats in College Green Ireland was allotted 100 at Westminster, a proportionately generous allowance in terms of the electorate. Some Anglo-Irish politicians survived the change and adapted themselves to their new environment, the most prominent being John Foster, the last speaker of the Irish Commons and a firm opponent of union. He was soon appointed to a ministerial position, though MPs at Westminster were reported to have been 'more astonished at the strength of Mr Foster's brogue than convinced by his arguments'.[16]

The failure to grant Catholic emancipation immediately after the union, as Pitt had quite sincerely promised, was undoubtedly the Achilles heel of the new union. It meant that government had reneged on its promise and that the members of the Anglo-Irish ascendancy continued to be the only Irish representatives at Westminster for the first three decades of the nineteenth century, until Daniel O Connell's mass popular movement forced emancipation on the union parliament in 1829. Thereafter repeal of the union, as John Foster and others had predicted in 1799 and 1800, became the objective of those who sought to harness or to redress political and social discontent.[17] The union need not have been a failure; the failure lay in the inability of its instigators, and those who succeeded them, to make it work generously or imaginatively.

8. The Death of the Irish Language

Richard B. Walsh

What do we mean when we say that a language is 'dead'?
People say, for instance, and readily believe, that Latin is a
'dead language'. Linguists could disagree amongst themselves
about this, depending on how they wish to understand the
words 'language' and 'Latin' and 'dead'. There ought to be
no need for us to get tangled up in intricacies of this kind here.
People who are in any way familiar with the steady decline
of the Irish language over the past three centuries or so, and
the gradual passing into history of the old Gaelic world to
which it belonged, will have a good idea as to what is implied
in the title of this talk.

Yet all around us we find disagreement as to whether the
Irish language is dead or dying; and there are those who
maintain that whatever its condition, the continued existence
of the Irish nation, as they conceive it, demands that the
language must, in some sense and by some means, be given
a new life as a national language, side by side with English,
in a bilingual state existing in a future which, because of the
facts of life and death, most of us will never see. Obviously
this projected re-birth could not be dealt with satisfactorily in
this modest essay, and we must be content with trying to
make what sense we can out of the known facts.

Speaking on RTE in 1968, the late Professor David Greene
said:

> When we say that a language is dying we are, of course, using a
> metaphor: what we mean is that most of the people who speak
> that language are beyond middle-age and that their children and
> grandchildren speak a different language.

This apparently simple explanation takes us a long way. On
that occasion Professor Greene went on to say:

If we look at Ireland a hundred years ago, we are immediately struck by the fact that the rate of change of language. . . from Irish to English, had no parallel anywhere in Europe, and hardly even in America, for it was being carried through in two generations rather than three.

During that hundred years the Irish language has figured in Irish nationalist ideology as being a feature of national distinctiveness. It was in the early twentieth century that the idea became firmly rooted, amongst those who were engaged in one way or another in the struggle for national independence, that a distinctively Irish nation–state was not possible without the Irish language.

Pearse articulated this idea very clearly, and his final desperate sacrifice was made for the resurrection of Gaelic Ireland. His own tireless dedication to the Irish language from his schooldays had, by about 1914, convinced him that, in the real world about him, in education, in literature, in politics, in the Church, there were few, far too few, who were prepared to follow him on the road he saw ahead. The Gaeltacht, which he knew so well, was melting away into the past before his eyes. The final sacrifice, in which he laid down his life, put the resurrection of Gaelic Ireland back into the metaphysical world from which it had come to him at the age of eighteen, when, in his first published words, he dedicated himself to a dream. Later, in his early twenties, writing in excellent Irish, which he had worked so very hard to learn, he told of this vision coming to him again as he sat gazing out over the sea in Connemara. What he wrote may be expressed briefly as follows: the old Gaelic world is not dead but only sleeping; the night will pass and the glorious dawn will come, the dawn of another golden age.

Pearse was a dreamer. But he was not an idle dreamer. He was a man of action, a man of extraordinary energy and dedication. He tried many forms of action towards the realisation of his dream. In the end the only action he could see left to him was the ultimate sacrifice, death. What he taught and what he did have had the effect of mesmerising more than one generation of Irish nationalists who have come after him.

By the time the new state was established, Pearse's dream

had become a national gospel. For many years no ambitious politician, whatever his real feelings about the language, could afford to ignore its reflection in the ballot-boxes. The idea that a distinctively Irish nation cannot be envisaged without the Irish language seems to be lurking shyly in the policy of the state at this moment. The reality is less and less in evidence as time goes on, and perhaps nowhere less evident than in the ordinary lives of those who legislate in its behalf.

This kind of nationalist doctrine did not, of course, originate in Ireland. Irish nationalism, including Irish linguistic nationalism, represents an attempt to adapt to the particular situation in Ireland one or other of the various forms of the idea of nationality and the nation-state which was playing a dominant role in European politics in the nineteenth century. Separate nationalities and nation-states had existed in Europe long before this time; but it was in the nineteenth century that aspirations towards national statehood and the establishment of independent political entities on the basis of nationalist philosophies took on a decisive role in designing the political map of Europe. It was in the nineteenth century also that the possession of a common ancestral language came to be an important criterion of national identity, though it must be remembered that there were also instances in which this linguistic criterion formed no part of the case of nations seeking self-determination. We often hear that the congruent political and cultural unity, which nowadays we see as characterising modern nation-states, did not exist in Gaelic Ireland. But this is also true of other places, like France, Germany, Italy, before the nineteeth century.

At an early stage in the adoption of nationalist political philosophies in Ireland, people like Thoman Davis, whose aim was a politically and economically independent state, came to believe that the language provided a reliable guarantee of separate identity and a barrier against its erosion by foreign influence. But Davis and his colleagues were far from advocating the Gaelic nation-state in Pearse's terms.

In the nineteenth century scholars like O'Donovan and O'Curry did a great deal to make the more educated people in Ireland aware of the Gaelic past. This provided sustenance for those who would argue that Ireland's claim to be a separate nation rested on its long and distinguished history as a cultural unity, with the Irish language continuing over many centuries as the language of life, literature and learning, and even as the language of the common bond of Christianity, across the tribal and territorial boundaries which marked what may be called the politics of Gaelic Ireland.

When the demand arose for the conversion of this ancient cultural unity into a modern political unity, into a new nation-state, it was natural that such people should see the survival of the Irish language as being essential to the kind of Irish nation they had in mind. We are talking about people who could not tolerate the idea of a new Irish state growing out of an English colony; who believed that continuity with the Gaelic past must be of the essence of the resurgent nation, and that the distinction, the very international status, of the new political entity must rest on its undisputed title to the inheritance of an ancient and prestigeous culture, guaranteed by the language.

What is very doubtful is whether the Irish language, as it stands today, can be seen as playing such a role in guaranteeing the international credit, in the strictly cultural sense, of the modern Irish state, or for that matter of the Irish nation, in the present or in the future. On the other hand, it is arguable that the title to the cultural inheritance has been firmly established, and that the medium through which it can best produce its effect is the English language. Like every other resource which this nation possesses, its effectiveness depends on the energy, commitment and sophistication of our own people.

While the vision of a Gaelic-speaking Irish nation-state was being promoted, mainly by urban-orientated people with a modern middle-class education and outlook, the last fragments of Gaelic Ireland, the foundation on which alone they could build, were crumbling away in bleak rural places, far removed from the middle-class scene, and, indeed, from the middle-class mind.

The story of the decline of Gaelic Ireland has been told over and over again. Mostly we find its progress measured in arithmetical terms: number and percentage of Irish speakers from one period to another. After the foundation of the new state the figures became deceptive, designed to include a new and mainly illusory category of 'Irish speakers'.

The bare numbers are enough to show that the position of the Irish language at the time when the Gaelic League was founded, in 1893, was such that any attempt to restore Irish as the numerically dominant language was up against overwhelming odds. Making some allowances for false declarations in the 1891 census (false declarations which, of themselves, are a symptom of the shattered nerve of Gaelic Ireland), a reasonable profile would look something like this: about eighty per cent of the people of Ireland could not speak Irish at all (or at least said they could not); and, of the remaining Irish-speaking population, about ninety per cent were bilingual.

But the numbers do not tell the whole story. Some of the most significant aspects of the decline of the language in the seventeenth and eighteenth centuries, when the fate of Gaelic Ireland was written on the wall, cannot be seen in terms of numbers alone. In the series of Thomas Davis lectures broadcast in 1966, the late Dr Maureen Wall contributed a classical account of the decline of the Irish language. A short passage from this very lucid paper will help to amplify what I have been saying:

> What was completely overlooked [by the revivalists] was the fact that before the nineteenth century began the Irish language had been banished from parliament, from the courts of law, from town and county government, from the civil service and from the upper levels of commercial life. By 1880 Irish had ceased to be habitually spoken in the homes of all those who had already achieved success in the world, or who had aspired to improve or even maintain their position politically, socially and economically. The pressures of six hundred years of foreign occupation, and more particularly the complicated political, religious and economic pressures of the seventeenth and eighteenth centuries, had killed Irish at the top of the social scale and had already weakened its position among the entire population of the country.

What is implied here is not so much that the revivalists were not aware of these facts – mostly they were; but rather that they failed to appreciate, or perhaps refused to admit, the depth of their significance, and that they preached and acted as if a few superficial adjustments could replace what had become firmly installed as the essential mechanism of Irish society.

By the early nineteenth century the Irish language had come to be associated with poverty, ignorance, social stagnation and political impotence. Those who could were anxious to grasp any opportunity of escaping from the cultural isolation (not to mention the economic disadvantages) inherent in belonging to an Irish-speaking community. The way out lay in getting some sort of modern, literate education, and particularly in learning English. The necessary education and the means of learning English were not then readily available to the masses of people who formed the Irish-speaking communities, but there is plenty of evidence that they were eager to take advantage of whatever means were within their reach. Here one cannot help remembering, amongst many other instances, the testimony of the great scholar, Eugene O'Curry. He spoke openly of his life-long regret at his lack of formal schooling, and he tells us how, as a youth in Co. Clare in the early years of the nineteenth century, he used to walk from his home in Doonaha into Kilkee to pick up what English he could from the summer visitors. Incidentally this is one of many instances which could be taken further to show that the determination to break through the linguistic barrier was not necessarily in conflict with the deep affection of the people for their native traditions.

It could be argued that, in assessing the decline of the Irish language in the nineteenth century, too much can be made of the mere reduction in the number of Irish speakers brought about by various forms of public action, whether by Church and State or by political movements. These factors were by now simply adding to an impetus which had long since developed a powerful momentum of its own. Some people may be shocked if I say that even in the case of the great Famine too much significance, in the particular context of this talk, could be attached to the mere reduction in the number of Irish speakers brought about by this national calamity, enormous as it was. Throughout the whole three centuries of decline, what needs to be seen as the constantly significant factor is the progressive relegation of the Irish-speaking community to cultural isolation, and the concomitant debasement of the status of its language as one of the living languages of Europe.

The story of the National Schools, which were instituted in the middle of the nineteenth century, is well known. Recent studies have emphasised the fact that they were no part of an English plan to kill the Irish language, a view which used to have some currency amongst misguided enthusiasts. By this time the English (if I may persist in the old ethnic idiom) had completed their part in this particular murder, and were satisfied to ignore the language, and, as it were, leave it 'for dead'. It was left to the surviving Irish-speaking communities to finish the job: using inhuman, weirdly determinist methods, they set out to kill their own native language on the spot. The story need not be repeated here: but it must be seen as reflecting the extremity to which Gaelic Ireland had been driven by more than two centuries of the cultural vandalism for which English colonialism since the seventeenth century will always be famous.

In the event, the process has taken longer than those bewildered people could have expected. Nobody denies that it is all but complete today. The revival movement came on a wave of romantic nationalist fervour; and, failing to read the signs, it drifted into one blind alley after another. Irish linguistic nationalism is making its last desperate stand against the most powerful international language in the world, and against the tide of international culture (to use this ambiguous term in its more technical sense), which engulfs the learned, the educated, the half-educated, the illiterate, the young and the old alike, across all the language barriers of the world, notably through the power of the English language.

It may be necessary to add here that we can no longer think of English as the language of the English, the 'old enemy'. Some people may be unwilling to accept this, in spite of many obvious realities including the reality of America. It has been demonstrated in a scholarly book by Professor Randolph Quirk, Vice-Chancellor of London University. He very neatly suggests that only an English crank would now claim the English language as the national property of the English.

It is not easy to say how many people would contend

seriously that the continued existence of the Irish nation, or of an Irish nation-state, depends on the role of the Irish language as envisaged in the latest plan of the revival movement. I think it is fair to ask what the language in this role could do to ensure the national dignity or the international status of the Irish people. It is easier to see an Irish state of the future, possibly embracing more than one Irish nation, which would guarantee the necessary self-respect and an acceptable international standing by means other than speaking Irish.

Already what may be called an Irish nation (admittedly in a sense never very clearly defined), using the English language as its own, has made the name of Ireland famous throughout the world, in a field which has always been, and, one hopes, always will be, one of the most rewarding pre-occupations of man, namely, creative literature.

This may be the point at which to recall the words of George Russell, who represents one of the many parts of that as yet unintegrated nation:

> We are less children of this clime
> Than of some nation yet unborn
> Or empire in the womb of time.
> We hold the Ireland in the heart
> More than the land our eyes have seen,
> And love the goal for which we start
> More than the tale of what has been.

What I mean by the 'death' of the Irish language is the end of the Gaeltacht, the passing of Gaelic Ireland into history. Those of us who have had the privilege of being very close to it in its last days would rather see it go with honour and dignity, and not, like poor Jack Falstaff, 'babbling of green fields'.

It happens that just at the time when Irish, as the living language of a community, had reached its final suicidal extremity, events were taking place which were to bring Gaelic Ireland and its language into prominence in the world of international learning: in linguistics, anthropology, literature, history. In 1853, the German linguist, Zeuss, published his *Grammatica Celtica*, which brought Celtic into the centre of Indo-European studies. By this time John

O'Donovan and Eugene O'Curry were approaching the end of those thirty years of dedicated scholarly labour by which they uncovered the riches of Gaelic Ireland for the whole world to see. The interest of scholars and creative writers in Gaelic Ireland, and in English-speaking Ireland, has grown since then, and is very active throughout the world today. In this, as in other fields of national activity, whatever claims we may base on the performance of our ancestors in the Gaelic past will depend for their validity on our own performance as the Irish of today.

As to our commitment to the nationalistic doctines we inherited from the nineteenth century, it may be well to reflect on the words of a man who wrote with great authority on the subject, the late Professor Alfred Cobban:

> At different times different institutions have embodied the political ideals of man. . . There is little to suggest that the combination of cultural and political unity in the idea of the nation state is the last, or that it is the highest, of those mortal gods to whom men have sometimes paid undue adoration. . . The state system of Europe has changed century by century, and there are no signs that its evolution has come to an end.

There is scarcely any subject under the sun which is so constantly beset by misconceptions, by fallacies, popular and otherwise, as language is. Some of the fallacies cannot really be called 'popular', since they have been found amongst the fundamental beliefs of people who are entrusted with the education of the young, and they have led to very undesirable results. Perhaps the most persistant and pervasive of these fallacies is the belief that, from a purely linguistic point of view, one language is better than another, or by the same principle, that one form of a particular language, say Standard English, is better than some other form, say Cockney or the Black English of American cities, in the sense that it is a more efficient medium for expression and understanding. Generally in the past this kind of attitude has been largely ignored by professional linguists as something inevitable and harmless. More recently, however, professional linguists have considered it necessary to demonstrate that this belief is not only false but also harmful in so far as it accounts for serious failures in the education of socially under-privileged children. It has been argued very convincingly that a language, or a dialect, is not *linguistically* inferior because it is the language of a socially disadvantaged community.

I mention this before concluding because the belief has been so widespread, amongst people who know little or nothing about language, that the Irish of the Gaeltacht became an inferior language because the people of the Gaeltacht became socially deprived and culturally isolated (it will be noted that I did not say 'culturally deprived', a very suspect notion in any context). This belief is quite false, and notably so in the case of Irish. There is an unpalatable irony in the fact that it has been common amongst the rank and file of revivalists.

Throughout this essay I have avoided purely linguistic considerations because they are not centrally relevant to the topic we are discussing. One language, or one form of a language, is popularly believed to be superior to another because it is used by people who enjoy higher social prestige, economic and political power, significant and far-reaching cultural influence. The story of the Irish language tells how it was gradually stripped of all these marks of social superiority. But social superiority and cultural superiority are quite different things (if I may insist on using the term 'culture' in its learned rather than its popular sense).

When I talk about the Irish language I mean the language of the Gaeltacht, the linguistic form in which the culture of Gaelic Ireland had been reflected and transmitted over centuries. Of this language and culture, especially through the use of modern technology in more recent years, we have vast records, not only in writing by also in sound. Scholars throughout the world are in little doubt about the value of this record of an important civilisation and an important language; not merely as a record confined to the domain of linguistics, anthropology or history, but as a source from which learning and art may draw for the enrichment of civilisations in the future and more particularly for the enrichment of whatever culture the Irish in the future may call their own. How this can be is by no means pure speculation; but it is a subject for a good deal of learned discussion far beyond the scope allowed us on this occasion.

No doubt many of you have heard the story of how a young girl from Co. Mayo, Margaret Burke Sheridan, took the formidable operatic world of Rome by storm with her conquering performance in *Madame Butterfly*, just at the time when Terence MacSweeney died in jail. Puccini may not belong to the top layer of operatic composers, but he was noted for sensitivity and evocation, and he said that God had told him to write only for the theatre. On this occasion he was astonished; and he was moved to ask himself how this young Irish girl could have glorified his music far beyond his own expectations. What he decided was that she could have done it only because she came of 'an old race full of dramatic temperament and spiritual vision'. The academic mind may shrink from this emotive pronouncement. Yet anybody who has known the living Gaeltacht intimately will be struck by the fortuitous aptness of Puccini's words, 'dramatic temperament and spiritual vision'. Sad and violent as Ireland was at that time, there cannot have been many occasions on which it was more appropriate to shout 'Up Mayo!' But the cry that lifted the roof of the opera house in Rome was 'Viva Irlanda'.

If people throughout the world are moved to cry out 'Viva Irlanda!', or its equivalent, naturally our hearts are warmed. We feel we are somebody and that we have something to offer to the world. Assuming that, for a long time to come, the political ideals of man will continue to be embodied in nation-states, then our standing in the world will depend on our performance in various fields both as a nation and as a state. It can scarcely be denied that the performance of a people, like the performance of a person, will always depend not only on the resources at its disposal but also on the wisdom with which it assesses the value of these resources, and on the energy, courage and confidence with which it applies itself to exploiting them.

I have tried to suggest, very tentatively I admit, and perhaps rather impressionistically, what may now be the value of the Irish language and the Gaelic inheritance in relation to the political and cultural aspirations of the Irish people.

9. Catholic Emancipation

Kevin B. Nowlan

Writing to a correspondent, in 1792, Edmund Burke, the great orator and advocate of Irish Catholic rights, observed of the Penal laws that they constituted 'a machine of wise and elaborate contrivance, and as well fitted for the oppression and impoverishment and degradation of a people and the debasement, in them, of human nature itself as ever proceeded from the perverted ingenuity of man'. Allowing for a certain measure of dramatic emphasis on his part, Burke focused attention on the quite extraordinary position of the Irish Roman Catholics even in the second half of the eighteenth century.

What gave the Irish Catholics a special position and gave to Irish political and social life a unique character was that alone of the European possessions of the British Crown, Ireland had a Roman Catholic majority, a majority which, however, did not control the real, substantial wealth of the country. As the late J. G. Simms put it in his valuable book, *The Williamite Confiscation in Ireland*, 'it may be reckoned that in the latter half of the eighteenth century some five thousand Protestant landlords owned nearly the whole of Ireland'. Catholic wealth, it is true, began to grow as the eighteenth century progressed, but the Protestant Ascendancy remained entrenched in the ownership of land and in the professions and the more lucrative branches of trade. This economic predominance had important social and political implications which were to influence the patterns of Irish life long after the eighteenth century had ended.

The term Catholic Emancipation has come, in general usage, to signify the dramatic developments which marked the closing years of the eighteen-twenties, but the Catholic Relief Act of 1829 was only the last in a succession of measures aimed at relieving Catholics from the legal penalties and restrictions imposed on them by the victors of the wars of the seventeenth century. The Catholic Relief Acts of 1778 and 1782, for example, had effectively put Catholics on the same footing as Protestants with regard to the ownership and inheritance of land – assuming that they had any to inherit. Again the 1782 Act liberalised the law respecting Catholic education and the registration of secular priests.

Things were changing. The French Revolution, the new tolerant ideas of the European Enlightenment, a somewhat bolder stance by the Irish Catholics themselves and the emergence among the Irish Protestants of radical and reforming elements inside and outside parliament were all factors encouraging and demanding more reforms. The Catholic Committee of 1792 was one symptom of this evolution and significantly Wolfe Tone was for a time assistant secretary to the Committee. In the political sphere, a radical and increasingly revolutionary expression of the new age were the Societies of United Irishmen who laid stress on the rights of all be they members of the Established Church, Catholics or Presbyterians.

The results of all these pressures, arguments and the fear of revolutionary unrest were the Catholic Relief Acts of 1792 and 1793, which removed almost all the remaining legal burdens from the Irish Catholics and they were admitted to the parliamentary franchise on the same footing as their Protestant neighbours. There was, however, one important reservation: Catholics were still excluded from membership of both houses of parliament so as to maintain it was argued, the Protestant Constitution and to guarantee the golden link between the crowns of Great Britain and Ireland.

The last decade in the life of Grattan's Parliament – a misleading title in view of Grattan's limited influence there – was to pass without any further concessions to Irish Catholic opinion, apart from the decision to found Maynooth College, at the instance of William Pitt, the British Prime Minister. The closing of the Irish colleges on the continent in the wake of the French revolutionary wars, prompted the hope, in official circles, that a state provision for the education of priests in Ireland would foster a measure of loyalty to the Crown in clerical circles at least. The annual grant to Maynooth was finally fixed at £8,000 but, even though it was a government proposal, it is symptomatic of the deep distrust of Catholicism in Ascendancy circles that the grant encountered bitter opposition from such powerful figures as Lord Clare, the Irish Lord Chancellor and one of the architects of the Union. On the other hand, the foundation of Maynooth and its endowment by the State could be seen as a first tentative move by the government towards giving the Catholic Church in Ireland something more than a grudging minimal measure of toleration.

The authorities in London had for some time contemplated the possibility of a Union of the two kingdoms, by bringing to an end the Parliament in Dublin and concentrating the whole business of legislation in London. The stormy events of 1798 and the fear of a separation between the two islands helped to seal the fate of the Dublin Parliament. Despite resistance from a variety of sources, the Irish Parliament voted itself out of existence. But though Dublin ceased to be a parliamentary capital, it remained after the Union as before the centre of administration for Ireland, an administation which continued to be dominated by the old Ascendancy. In some ways little had changed, but the debates and controversy surrounding the Union had aroused expectations in Irish Catholic circles that, within the new United Kingdom, the final barriers of a political kind would be removed and Catholics would be enabled to sit in either House of Parliament – a gesture of some importance, it was believed, in helping the Irish Catholics of property to advance towards a real measure of equality of status with their Protestant fellow countrymen.

Though Daniel O'Connell and others like him deplored the ending of the old Irish Parliament, many influential Catholics, including members of the hierarchy, tended to be indifferent or even hopeful of better times to follow, an expectation strongly encouraged by the predictions of the British government. In fact, however, the Union was not followed by speedy concessions to Catholic aspirations, in political, or indeed social, terms, but rather by a decade or more of prevarications and frustrations which were made no easier by the economic difficulties which followed the ending of the Napoleonic Wars and by the widespread problems of poverty and rural unrest in Ireland. The Union seemed to offer no great rewards either in terms of Catholic Emancipation or economic advance. The opportunity of reconciling a significant sector of Irish Catholic opinion to the Union and to a closer identification with Great Britain was being lost through indecision on the part of government and through the persistence of a deep-rooted anti-Catholic feeling among influential elements in Britain, including King George III and his successor George IV.

Politically the power of the Protestant landed class remained secure in the immediate post-Union period. Though Catholics had been given the parliamentary franchise, landlord influence and the limited number of contested elections ensured that the Catholic vote would remain, at least for a time, of little practical consequence. Quickly many of those who had opposed the Union, because it might lead to an increase in Catholic influence, came to see in it instead a guarantee of the continued influence and authority of the landed Ascendancy. Yet the Catholic problem would not go away nor could the fear of political and agrarian unrest in the countryside be readily forgotten.

The annual grant to Maynooth, the discreet discussions between government and conservative Catholics at the time of the Union all helped to create a new atmosphere and to open up the possibility of a new relationship between the Roman Catholic Church and the State, once the Union had been accomplished. It was argued that in the United Kindom of the future, the Irish Catholics would always be in a minority and could pose, therefore, no real threat to the Protestant character of the British Constitution. Further, if somehow the Catholic Church could be brought into some formal link with the state, its potentially dangerous power could be contained. Some such connection between the Catholic Church and the state had many attractions for government. By, say, providing salaries, from public funds, for the bishops and parish clergy, they would be made more amenable to official influence and the old fear of the rebellious, difficult and independent Irish priest would be banished for ever. Better still would be for the government to have a measure of control over the appointment of the bishops, thereby lessening, too, the risk of papal interference in the British dominions. And in this connection it must be remembered that in many European countries, even in some predominantly Protestant ones, the State had a role in the process of appointing Roman Catholic bishops.

In the years before and after 1800, therefore, the view took shape in certain circles that Catholic Emancipation could be safely granted and Protestant fears be put at rest, provided the British crown had some kind of veto over episcopal and other senior appointments and this suggestion was usually linked with the proposition to endow the Catholic Church as perhaps a kind of lesser establishment alongside the official Established Church.

On the Catholic side, on the eve of the Union, the Irish bishops or a considerable number of them, had shown a willingness to go along with an informal offer by the British Government to pay the clergy a stipend in return for the right of the Crown to confirm ecclesiastical appointments. Then in 1814, Monsignor Quarantotti, of the Congregation for the Propagation of the Faith, influenced, it seems, by English Catholic opinion, issued an official statement, a rescript, favouring the granting of the veto to the British Crown. Though some Irish Catholics and friends of Emancipation like Henry Grattan supported such a proposal, the terms of the Roman rescript provoked a storm of opposition in Ireland, among clergy and laity alike. An easy acceptance of state patronage, especially from what was regarded as a Protestant state had already become most unlikely. In contrast to the Catholic Church in other European countries, the special circumstances in Ireland were such as to make the concept of a Church free of the state the desirable one, and the one to be fought for in the Emancipation campaign. Not surprisingly, those who rejected a state provision for the Catholic Church would also see in the special status of the Protestant Established Church, supported by tithes, a further source of grievance in the years ahead.

The stiffening of the Irish opposition to state interference in Church affairs gave a new sharpness and purpose to the agitation for Emancipation in the eighteen-twenties and focused attention on the dramatic impact of Daniel O'Connell on the Irish scene. The Emancipation campaign had tended to languish in the immediate post-Union years. The Catholic voice was weak, opposition to Emancipation in Parliament was still considerable and on the Veto issue Catholics were divided. However, even as early as 1808, the Irish bishops had second thoughts about the Veto and, by a majority, rejected it as inexpedient. By 1814, the time of the Quarantotti rescript, the bishops had become bold enough to reject it as not binding in practice. But it needed a new leadership to give the Emancipation movement a fresh purpose and to strengthen the resolve of the Irish Church to reject firmly any proposal to make the Church dependent on the State. In that growing radicalism could be seen, I believe, an early expression of an Irish identity confronted by the challenge of continued assimilation into an English world.

It would, however, be wrong to assume that the movement away from timid representations to vigorous popular agitation in the Emancipation cause took place overnight. The Catholic Board, already riven by a power struggle between the old, cautious, genteel leadership, and the new radicals, had been suppressed by a government fearful that the radicals would prevail. It was not really until a new Catholic Association was set up in 1823 that the prospects began to brighten. The dogged ultra-Tory resistance to Emancipation, the toughening of the Catholic attitude and a widespread sense of frustration about social and economic problems, all helped the rise of Daniel O'Connell, but, in his turn, his energy, sense of timing and his power to hold the people with his oratory and ability to join the Emancipation issue to wider grievances, gave a new impulse to the Catholic movement. The basis of the agitation was, in effect, being widened in social and political terms.

Yet the Catholic Association of 1823 started on a rather low key. It needed the brilliant proposal made by O'Connell to invite the people of Ireland, the poor as well as the better off, to enroll as associate members by paying one penny a month – the Catholic Rent – to alter the whole character of the movement. As the historian of the Emancipation agitation, James Reynolds, put it: 'The beginning of the Rent marks the transition of the Catholic Association from a small club into a mass movement.' O'Connell and his supporters, and he won the strong backing of the clergy, made the Emancipation a symbol of much more – of the need to raise the status of the ordinary people, of the need for justice and, in effect, the curtailment of the power of the Ascendancy. The success of this remarkable agitation very soon alarmed the Government in London.

O'Connell made mistakes and some disliked the emphatic, robust style of his oratory, but he drew the crowds and the influence of the Association and the size of the Catholic Rent continued to grow. In 1825, however, he came near enough to serious trouble. Not merely was the Catholic Association suppressed by the authorities, but he was induced, in London, by some friends of Emancipation to support a Catholic relief bill which had, as was said, two 'wings' to it, so as to make it more acceptable to Parliament. It was proposed that a state payment be made to the Catholic clergy and that the forty-shilling freehold franchise be abolished. The bill, in fact, came to grief in Parliament. That O'Connell should have supported a measure which could be seen as a retreat from his advocacy of a wide popular franchise and Church rights provoked considerable criticism in Ireland. O'Connell, however, quickly retrieved his position and even contrived to re-establish a Catholic Association and evade the legal prohibitions on such movements. The case for an independent Church and full emancipation was reasserted. The way was open for the extraordinary triumphs of the years between 1826 and 1829.

Profiting from the strength of the pro-Emancipation lobby in Parliament, and it must never be forgotten, the growing instability of the Tory government, O'Connell and the Association skilfully exploited the possibilities of mass organisation, of demonstrating that the country voters, given the proper leadership, could be induced to rebel against their landlords and vote for candidates, who, though Protestant, were favourable to Emancipation. In a rough and ready way, an advance was being made towards democratic participation in the process of government and this almost as much as the demand for Emancipation alarmed the authorities in Dublin and London. The reputation of O'Connell as a liberal pioneer of popular political representation was being established and friends of free institutions in Britain and on the continent were quick to grasp the significance of what was happening in Ireland. It was becoming apparent, too, that one could be a liberal and, at the same time, an advocate of Catholic rights, a strange combination for many continentals in the wake of the anti-clericalism of the French Revolution.

Election victories, like those in Waterford and Louth, were phases in the shaping of popular political participation, but it needed the Clare Election, of June 1828, to demonstrate in an unambiguous way that the Irish Catholics could be an effective political force without recourse to an openly violent defiance of the state. A rival Ascendancy to the Protestant one was at least potentially there, and this was not lost on contemporary observers.

The agitation created an enthusiasm and a determination in the countryside which seriously troubled the Duke of Wellington and Robert Peel. They feared that the agitation might end in violence or even rebellion. Troops were drafted into the country, but there was little the ministers could do except watch O'Connell, Wyse, Sheil and the rest orchestrate the elections and organise the protection of those voters who were willing to defy their landlords. There was an anxiety, too, in government circles that Emancipation could develop into a demand for the Repeal of the Act of Union, which was of course O'Connell's other great objective. Emancipation, O'Connell said, in 1828, would reconcile Ireland to England, but, he warned, 'if it is not carried soon these countries will certainly separate' – a prospect no British statesman could contemplate with equanimity.

There was a dread of rebellion in official circles and a fear that O'Connell could not maintain popular discipline for ever. Peel, though long opposed to Emancipation and detesting O'Connell, was an able and pragmatic man. He began to think increasingly in terms of a quick settlement with the Catholics. It is, I think, fair to say that the Clare Election resolved the immediate situation for him and Wellington and they dragged a reluctant King George IV along with them.

What made the Clare Election so remarkable was that a Catholic took the bold step of standing for election, knowing that under the law he could not take his seat in Parliament if elected. Daniel O'Connell was the candidate. No suitable Protestant could be found to oppose in this by-election the popular Vesey FitzGerald, one of the more liberal supporters of the government. Reluctantly at first and then with growing enthusiasm, O'Connell agreed to stand. With that enthusiasm grew the will of the electorate to vote for him. Their discipline and resolution were impressive and so was the result of the election: 2,057 votes for Dan O'Connell, 982 for FitzGerald.

Even before the Clare Election, Robert Peel saw the situation in Ireland as 'much worse than open rebellion'. His answer was a clear and decisive one, namely the Catholic Relief Bill of 1829. The Duke and Peel used all their influence to get it through Parliament. Many Tories hated the measure, but the alternative to passing it was the fall of the government. By April 13, Emancipation had became law.

What was this Relief Act and what did it signify for Ireland in the years after 1829? The old objectionable oaths were replaced by one which Catholics could subscribe to. This enabled them to sit in Parliament and hold all public offices except such posts as regent or lord lieutenant of Ireland. And though the remainder of the Act was largely a dead letter, it recalled the old suspicions of Popery by providing that all religious services had to be indoors, that Catholic bishops could not use territorial titles and that any member of a religious order entering the United Kingdom could be deported.

As such the Act granted little that was directly relevant to the social and economic needs of the mass of the people. But to leave the comment at that point would be to lose an important perspective. Under the leadership of O'Connell, Wyse, Sheil and the clergy, the potential of the organised voters was displayed for the first time in Ireland. It was an exercise in extra-parliamentary pressure of a planned kind. It showed that the power of the Ascendancy and of the Crown could be effectively challenged. A pioneering exercise in the popular will, the Emancipation campaign was to provide the precedent for the repeal agitation of the eighteen-forties and the Home Rule movement of a still later time. It was part of the long process in political education and its influence was to be seen as well in Britain in the eighteen-thirties and forties and in the Catholic liberal associations in Germany, France and Italy.

Emancipation, too, was achieved without linking the Irish Catholic Church with the state as some had sought to accomplish. The way in which the movement had evolved – the assertion of the principle of a separation between Church and state was to be of enormous long-term significance for the Church in its relations with the people, with the nationalist movements and with future governments.

But there was another dimension to this rejection of any connection with the state. Professor Kennedy Roche, of Cork, has made the point that, in practice, the Emancipation campaign 'made a massive contribution to a new theory of Church-State relationships; the experience of Ireland and Great Britain combined with those of the British colonies and the United States supplied virtually the entire factual. . . basis of the new Catholic liberal theory which was for long, at Rome, a political heresy'.

Unhappily the Relief Act was accompanied by a measure to abolish the forty-shilling franchise which had given the farming community the vote. The government could not risk a repetition of the Clare Election. In retrospect, it is clear that O'Connell and his friends made a mistake in not resisting strongly the abolition of this franchise. They may have felt that it would have been impossible, in the long-term, to stave off the influence of the landlords on the voters, or to maintain the kind of enthusiasm which made the Emancipation campaign possible. In practice, the end of the forty-shilling franchise robbed the popular party of a significant part of its electoral base. The events of the eighteen-forties were to show how difficult it was to build up an effective Repeal party in Parliament despite the strong and widespread support for Repeal in Ireland, for the restoration of an Irish parliament. It was to need the massive reform of the electoral system, in the late nineteenth century, to bring about a lasting improvement in terms of popular representation at Westminster.

The Emancipation campaign had about it the promise of Catholic, popular political power. And while it did not, in itself, go far towards toppling the structure of Ascendancy, it was a step along a road which was to bring with it new problems, especially in terms of what constitutes an Irish national identity and how groups with different traditions can seek a community of purpose, politically or otherwise.

The examination of, say, the pattern of political development during the years of the Repeal agitation shows that already it was becoming difficult for many to distinguish between what were Catholic aspirations and what constituted the valid nature of Irish nationalism. It is true that O'Connell claimed that among Repealers the question asked was 'not to what religion he belongs, but whether he is a true-born Irishman'. The Young Irelanders were, indeed, to criticise O'Connell because of the strength of Catholic clerical influences in the Repeal Association, but they were hardly much more successful, with their concept of an all-embracing Irish nationality, in winning any significant support among members of the Established Church, or, indeed, among the Presbyterians of the North despite their more radical tradition.

Individuals from the Protestant communities were to play a notable part in the leadership and shaping of Irish political and cultural movements in the later nineteenth century, but the inevitable rise of Catholic power and ambitions, in the decades after 1829, brought with it both a decline in Protestant privilege and a new fear, namely that one ascendancy would be replaced by another. Historical problems are never easy ones.

10. The Land War

Joseph Lee

'The Land War' is actually something of a misnomer for the struggle for the land in the nineteenth century. The term, it is true, entered popular consciousness, and historians use it as a convenient shorthand. But it is misleading insofar as it implies that there was only one type of land war when there were at least three separate, though overlapping, types. The first is the familiar one that pitched farmers in general against landlords in general. That is the land war that has been co-opted onto the official nationalist platform, the 'good' land war, replete with its consoling cast of heroes and villains. The second type of conflict was that within the farming class itself, between small farmers and graziers. Some small farmers, particularly in the west, took the view that the ranches should be redistributed in the interest, naturally, of the small farmers clinging around the edge. The resonances of that conflict would echo well into the twentieth century, to be exploited by the vaguely redistributionist rhetoric of Fianna Fáil in the 1930s and of Clann na Talmhan in the 1940s. That type of confrontation did not fit quite so comfortably into the nationalist pantheon of safe causes. It did, after all, involve conflict within the axiomatically united ranks. Nevertheless it was generally smothered in the capacious folds of the green flag or muted through the 'hush money' of the farmers dole, a small price to pay for keeping men with time on their hands – and time was one commodity they had in abundance – from asking awkward questions.

The third type of land war raised more awkward issues still, so awkward that the only safe course was amnesia. That was a conflict between agricultural labourers and cottiers, on the one hand, and stronger farmers on the other. That conflict loomed large before the Great Famine of 1846-1850. But it has since been consigned to almost total oblivion in the popular mind. In fact, however, so far as we can tell, a substantial proportion of the total agrarian outrages recorded on the eve of the Famine were perpetrated by labourers on farmers. In the thirty years before the Famine, strong farmers tried to shift from tillage to pasture as livestock prices rose faster than grain prices. It was a natural reaction on their part to price movements. The agricultural labourers and the cottiers, who made up more than half the population, desperately needed land for the potatoes that formed their staple diet. The labourers relied heavily on conacre from the better off farmers to grow their potatoes. This was a different type of conacre from that familiar to us today. The stronger farmer generally rented very small plots, often less than an acre, to the labourer. The farmer cast impatient eyes on this land as livestock prices became more remunerative. But the labourers waged a desperate resistence campaign, frequently punctuated by outrage against farmers who tried to raise conacre rents or reduce conacre lettings.

Some of the best known secret societies of the time, like the Terryalts in Clare, were more concerned with curbing farmers than landlords. The conflict had reached ugly proportions by the 1840s, but the Famine now solved the problem for the farmers at a stroke. The Great Famine from 1846–1950 was the worst natural catastrophe to strike Western Europe in the nineteenth century. Out of a total population of eight and a half million, perhaps more than a million people died, and died horribly, from hunger and disease. Another million emigrated during the Famine itself and in the years immediately following. But the Famine did not affect everybody equally. There were winners as well as losers in the famine stakes. The main losers, inevitably, were the small men, labourers and the cottiers, while the main winners were the stronger farmers.

Most of the famine dead were labourers and cottiers in the west and south of the country. The number of labourers and cottiers fell from more than one million in 1845 to less than 600,000 in 1851. The number of farmers over fifteen acres actually rose somewhat, from about 277,000 to 290,000. The balance of population and power changed significantly in rural Ireland in those few years.

Conacre was useless to labourers when the potato failed.

The conacre and cottier plots had to be thrown up, and were almost wiped out in a few years. Stronger farmers pounced on the chance to snatch back at least half a million acres, probably more nearly a million, over which they had lost effective control. Another million and a half acres came on the market through the death or emigration or eviction of the cottiers and small farmers. It was the landlords who owned this land, but as the holdings fell vacant they generally rented them out again to bigger farmers who were in a position to pay their rent and who were therefore able to increase the size of their own holdings. If the number of farms over fifteen acres – and fifteen acres remember was a fair sized farm in many parts of the country in 1850 – barely rose during the Famine, the average effective size of those farms rose sharply when more than two million acres became providentially available. Most of the stronger farmers, therefore, were able to do rather well out of the Famine.

The ten thousand landlords enjoyed mixed fortunes. Some seized with relish the opportunity offered by the Famine to clear their lands of big numbers of cottiers who were virtual squatters from the landlord point of view. Others found their rent plunging when their tenants couldn't pay. These landlords often went bankrupt, particularly if they themselves had big mortgages and other heavy expenses, or were already seriously in dept. About one-seventh of the land of Ireland was auctioned off in the Encumbered Estates Court during the decade after the Famine on behalf of landlords who could not meet their commitments. On the other hand, the stronger landlords, like the stronger farmers, did well. They recovered land from cottiers and small farmers who had frequently fallen into arrears, and rented out the land again to bigger farmers who could pay regularly. The landlords did not usually raise the actual rent to any great extent, but they now had more solvent tenants and were therefore assured of more reliable payment. And farmers did find it reasonably easy to pay rents in the thirty years after the Famine. Livestock prices and butter prices rose sharply between 1847 and 1877. These rising prices diffused unprecedented prosperity throughout the countryside. Small farmers were still, of course, very poor by later standards, but they were better off, and often much better off, than ever before, and their condition improved pretty steadily. They became accustomed for the first time to expecting improvement as the natural order of things.

It was not only the farmers who now expected things to keep getting better. So did the shopkeepers and the publicans who gave them long credit on their purchases. Many small farmers got into debt for the first time after the Famine because it was the first time the shopkeepers felt they were a safe enough risk for a loan. In social terms too, even smaller farmers became a bit more secure. The gap between themselves and the labourers was widening, and they could derive quiet satisfaction from their enhanced status.

Even the small farmer, therefore, was feeling fairly smug in 1877, thirty years after black '47. But in 1877 circumstances suddenly changed for the worse. The potato crop failed badly. That did not in itself create a crisis. It usually took two successive failures, or two bad failures out of three, for a real crisis to develop. And there was some recovery in the potato crop in 1878. But it was still only a middling year. Then in 1879 the potato failed catastrophically. Small farmers fell deep into arrears with their rents. Evictions nearly trebled between 1877 and 1879. In 1880 the potato recovered throughout most of the country. But it failed badly again in Connaught. The west generally, therefore, suffered a run of four poor potato crops in a row. In addition, cattle and butter prices fell for the first time in several years due to the slump in Britain, the main Irish market. Shopkeepers' debts could not be paid. Farmers who had accumulated fairly heavy debts in the '70s now confronted a real crisis as they came under pressure from the landlord on the one hand, and from the shopkeepers on the other. As Professor Baldwin told the Richmond Commission in 1882:

> People have been from a variety of remote causes deficient in thrift, then has come the great bound of modern prosperity. The greater wealth led to the establishment of a great many banks. The banks gave money on easy terms to shopkeepers and then the shopkeepers, as it were, forced a system of credit upon the small farmer and all of a sudden that has collapsed.

Other factors exacerbated the problems of potato failure.

America and England were plunged into deep slump between 1873 and 1879. The flow of emigrant remittances back home declined to a trickle, and emigration from Ireland fell sharply. Intense frustration built up among the surplus children cooped up at home.

The question arises, however, why was it in Mayo that the classic Land War of 1879–82 first broke out. Mayo had not been particularly prominent in previous agrarian agitations. But Mayo now suffered from additional afflictions, or at least experienced some peculiar circumstances. Probably about 5,000 extra young men were precluded from emigrating by the American slump. They sought some compensation in joining their brothers in seasonal migration to Britain to work on the harvest there. But the British harvest also failed badly at the end of the '70s, depriving Mayo of that particular safety valve for the suppressed energies of its young men. The failure of the potato crop after 1877 also affected every other sector of the rural economy in the west. It particularly affected pigs and poultry in Mayo. This was important because not only did it lose money for the farmers but it made the women restless. Women had generally been losers in the famine stakes. Domestic industry, especially spinning, from which many had earned a meagre pittance before the Famine, finally collapsed. Most women were left with no independent source of income. They had to become more subservient to their husbands or fathers or brothers. Women's major ally after the Famine was the hen. The number of hens grew by leaps and bounds once the coming of the railway to Mayo after 1860 allowed eggs to be taken more quickly to urban markets. Eggs were women's business. The number of fowl increased more quickly in Mayo than anywhere else in the country and Mayo women were singularly sensitive to vibrations in the egg market.

Circumstances were still far better than thirty years before, of course, and the government, like the landlords, balked at admitting the extent of the problem. If the natives had not become obstructive during the Famine, so their thinking ran, why should they become agitated now? One answer was that their expectations had changed as their circumstances had improved during the intervening period. They were no longer resigned to the inscrutable decrees of an all wise providence. The farmers were indignant because the run of good years had come to an abrupt end and they were often in debt. The farmers' children were indignant because both seasonal and permanent emigration was dammed up. The farmers' wives were indignant because on top of everything else the bottom was falling out of the egg market. The timber was dry. But it still needed someone to put a spark to it. It was at this psychologically crucial moment Michael Davitt returned to Mayo.

Davitt had been born into a small Mayo farm in 1846. His father was soon evicted, and Davitt was forced to emigrate with his family to England. He duly became a Fenian, and was sent to jail in 1870. Having suffered horribly in prison, he was released on a ticket of leave in 1877. He then went to America to see his mother. There he learned of the growing concern about the land situation among the Irish Americans.

Many Irish-American leaders were much closer to the ordinary Irish-American than were the bulk of political leaders in Ireland to the ordinary Irish. Even most Home Rule MPs of the time were drawn from the higher social classes, and had little personal knowledge of the condition of the small farmers. In America, however, many immigrant leaders had a lively sense of the difficulties at home. Davitt felt the ground-swell among the Irish in America on the land issue, and when he returned to Mayo in 1878 and saw the situation at first hand he quickly decided to make the land question central to agitation. He also realised that if he did not, others would. The main local leader at the time was James Daly, editor of the *Connaught Telegraph*. A well known figure in the county, Daly was instrumental in publicising tenant grievances, and in stiffening tenant resolve that there would be no repetition of the Great Famine. But he was no Fenian, and Davitt felt the need to move quickly. But he was obliged initially to co-operate in loose alliance with the popular Daly. It was Daly who organised the famous meeting in Irishtown on 20 April 1879, the first great public meeting of the land movement. When this proved successful in achieving its immediate objective of forcing a local landlord to reduce rents, the agitation gained momentum.

In August Davitt launched the Land League of Mayo. In October he was instrumental in establishing the National Land League. A bitter and a violent struggle had already broken out at grassroots level in an attempt to reduce rents and limit the growing number of evictions. Recorded outrages rose from 300 in 1878 to 4,400 in 1881. Many of these consisted simply of threatening letters, which might or might not frighten landlords, or bailiffs, or tenants who were warned not to rent land from which others had been evicted. But there were also frequent assaults, and some cases of torture and murder. The initial outbreaks in the west owed relatively little to national leadership. They were a response by the local tenantry under local leaders to local pressures. But they were quickly nationalised, so to speak, by Davitt and increasingly by Charles Stuart Parnell, through the Land League. Some particularly callous evictions, like those at Ballagh in Mayo in 1879, or the Murroe evictions by Lord Cloncurry in Limerick in 1880 (one of the children evicted at Murroe was destined to become Fr John Hayes the founder of Munitir na Tíre), fanned the flames. The technique of boycott, which Parnell and Davitt strongly advocated, achieved wide publicity for the League. Agitation spread through other counties in the south and east. But these were not generally small farm counties like Mayo. It was now a more prosperous tenantry, in many cases strong farmers and even graziers, who became actively involved as they sniffed the chance of reducing their own rents by manipulating the agitation begun by the small farmers of the west.

The Land League virtually abandoned Connacht as soon as it secured wider support. The publicity surrounding the Captain Boycott affair in the winter of 1880 disguised the fact that the Land League was pulling out of Mayo, leaving the awkward small farmers who were clamouring for redistribution of graziers' land to their fate. The League now had too much to lose to be seen to be in collusion with demands for redistribution of grazier lands, so subversive of the social order. Parnell wiped the clay of Connacht off his feet as soon as it had served his opportunistic purpose. Evictions actually rose in Mayo in 1880 and 1881 whereas they fell in the strong farmer areas on which the Land League was now concentrating.

William Gladstone, the English Prime Minister, eventually responded to the agitation with a major land act in 1881. This act set up land courts which adjudicated on the tenant claims for rent reductions. In most cases the courts reduced rents immediately by around 20%. The tenant could now appeal to the courts against the rent demanded by the landlord, and he could no longer be evicted as long as he paid the rent recommended by the courts. It was a major step forward. But it had one serious drawback. Only tenants who were not in arrears on their rent payments were eligible to apply. The act, therefore, favoured the stronger farmers who could afford to pay their rents and discriminated against the small farmers who could not. Those who were last to climb on the band wagon reaped the first benefits.

Nearly two-thirds of the Mayo tenantry remained in arrears, ground down by a succession of bad harvests. The act was no use to them. Little wonder that outrages actually increased after the land act. The accelerating tempo of terror in the countryside induced Gladstone to accept Parnell's plea that legislation should be introduced to extend the benefits of the land act to tenants in arrears. This arrears act of 1882 and not the land act of 1881 was the first major measure passed by parliament that benefited Irish small farmers.

There remained, however, one weakness in this arrangement from a tenant viewpoint. The tenant could still be evicted if he failed to pay the rent as assessed by the court. When agricultural prices fell sharply again by about 30% in 1886 and 1887 many tenants were unable to pay. Evictions increased. So did agitation though it never quite recovered the crescendo of the Land League years. Tim Harrington, editor of the *Tralee Chronicle* and a leader of the Land Movement in Kerry, initiated the Plan of Campaign in 1886 to counter the new threat. Under this scheme tenants on an estate offered the landlord what they considered a fair rent. If he refused, they combined to withhold all rents and then used the money to support any tenants whom the landlord evicted. The plan was put into effect on more than a hundred estates. The tenants showed an impressive solidarity. So did the landlords. They fought back vigorously and formed their own consortium to confront tenant solidarity with landlord solidarity. The most famous case occurred on the Smith-Barry estate in Tipperary, where the tenant leaders went to the extreme step of founding the town of New Tipperary in 1890 in a futile attempt to bring Arthur Hugh Smith-Barry, a formidable leader of the landlord syndicate, to his knees. The Plan of Campaign was generally fought to a bitter draw in the 1890s.

Tenants continued to lose occasional battles throughout the '90s. But time was on their side. The government became convinced that only by buying out the landlords could social peace be established in Ireland and the Union consolidated. The Ashbourne Act of 1885, the Balfour Act of 1891, the Wyndham Act of 1903, further amended in 1909, permitted tenants to buy out the landlords, through loans from the government on increasingly attractive terms. Rents might have fallen to some extent in any case, in response to market pressures, during the agricultural depression of the 1880s. With the recovery in agricultural prices from the mid-1890s, rents would have risen quite sharply again if market pressures were permitted to dominate. The Wyndham Act was a decisive one in the struggle for power between landlord and tenant. Before 1903 about 70,000 holdings were purchased by their tenants. Nearly 300,000 were bought under the Wyndham Act. The ownership of rural Ireland changed hands in a generation as peasant proprietorship superseded landlordism.

Michael Davitt celebrated *The Fall of Feudalism* as he called his famous book published in 1904. But peasant proprietorship had not been his own favoured solution originally. He preferred land nationalisation. The title to the land would be vested in the state and the land would be held by the tenants from the state. In Davitt's scheme the tenant would be left in secure possession as long as he satisfied some standard of efficiency. Davitt felt that land really belonged to the community and therefore the tenant held it in trust for the community and had a duty to farm it reasonably efficiently. The farmers were not impressed. There would be no nonsense about efficiency as far as they were concerned. It was not the business of anybody else, the state or the public, or Michael

Davitt or any other interfering busy-body what they did with their land. They had not fought the land war to be crucified on the cross of efficiency.

The outcome of the war therefore consolidated the existing property distribution and strengthened the men of property yet further against the men of no property. The man with 300 acres continued to hold his 300 acres. The man with 30 acres held his 30 acres. The man with nothing continued to hold his nothing. This actually widened the gap between the men of landed property, however small, and the remaining agricultural labourers. The 'haves', though it was not much that some of them had, became owners on favourable terms. The 'have nots' remained 'have nots' on the same terms as before.

Peasant proprietorship was simultaneously a social revolution and a social counter-revolution. It crowned the stong farmer as the cock of the country walk. Within half a century he had, on the one hand, repulsed the threat from below, from the cottier and labourer, and on the other hand he had smashed the threat from above, from the landlords. Through the workings of a benevolent providence, his two great enemies had been destroyed for him. The Famine had broken the spirit of the labouring class, apart from an occasional flash of indignation. The landlords had been destroyed by an agitation begun in the far west by small farmers. But it was the stronger farmers who managed to scoop most of the winnings after they had belatedly appropriated the movement when they grasped its potential.

There were still about 400,000 of them left in 1880. They were down to 300,000 by 1910. A hundred thousand labourers vanished during the thirty years when the official land war was being won. They would continue to dwindle into virtual extinction in the following half century. The small farmers themselves, the last possible rural threat to the hegemony of the stronger farmers would begin to follow the labourers until they too seemed well on the way to extinction half a century after their apparent victory in the land war. The children of the small farmers continued to take the emigrant ship. Their fathers' farms held as little hope for them after the land war as before. In 1883, four years after Irishtown, three years after the retreat of Captain Boycott, a year after the arrears act, Mayo experienced the heaviest emigration of any year since the great Famine. The propagandists who blamed the landlord system for the low output of Irish agriculture won the political and polemical battle. But political rhetoric could make little impression on economic reality. The decline in landlordism led to no significant increase in the economic performance of agriculture. History would belie the fond predictions that 'the fall of feudalism' in Ireland would bring forth a land flowing with milk and honey.

11. The Founding of the Gaelic League

Donal McCartney

When seven men met in a room in Lower O'Connell Street to found the Gaelic League, they were starting, according to Pearse, not a revolt but a revolution. The original Gaelic Leaguers (and Hyde's Diary stated that there were ten or twelve men present not seven), saw themselves not so much as revolutionaries but as conservationists, whose primary objective was to keep the Irish language spoken in Ireland. In so far as the Gaelic League soon proposed to teach Irish to those who knew none, it was in fact launching a counter-revolution, in an attempt to stem the massive tide of Anglicisation which had overtaken the country. As its strength and confidence grew, the Gaelic League began to urge the de-anglicisation of Ireland. Nothing less than revolution – linguistic and ultimately political revolution – became the objective of those who in Pearse's phrase, 'had been to school to the Gaelic League'.

If we were to take into account a perspective larger than that offered by Pearse, there would be a sense in which it might be argued that the much deeper revolution began, not with the attempt to preserve Irish, but rather with the earlier abandonment of the language by a people determined to achieve modernisation. For centuries, Irish had been the language of the country. By the beginning of the nineteenth century, however, the most glorious years of Gaelic literature were long past, and spoken Irish was retreating fast from the linguistic map of Europe.

Census returns on the state of the language have always to be treated with caution. Even today, a person with an extremely limited knowledge of Irish may claim to be able to speak it. In mid-nineteenth century Ireland, the opposite was the case, and many with little facility in English, liked to be able to boast of their knowledge of it. But allowing for the subjectivity of replies upon which Census figures are based, the general picture would appear to be something like this: in 1841, immediately before the Great Famine, about 50% of a population of over eight million people, spoke Irish. Ten years later, in 1851, this had been reduced to 23.3%. By 1891, just before the Gaelic League was founded, a mere 14.5% of the population claimed to be able to speak Irish.

Remorseless erosion of the language had begun long before the twin nineteenth-century tragedies of the Great Famine and the subsequent emigration increased the rate of change. It was once fashionable, but far too simplistic, to put the blame on O'Connell and the National Schools between them for the wiping out of the language. Long before a National school was built in any part of the country, and long before O'Connell appealed to the forty shilling freeholders of Waterford and Clare for their votes in the Emancipation struggle, the children of the country were eagerly learning English in their own hedge schools and at the insistence of their Irish-speaking parents. Some idea of the inroads made by English can be gauged by the fact that if we take Westmeath in the very heart of the country, we find that in the whole of that county in 1851 there was only one person in the total population of 111,000 who spoke Irish only; 920 persons in the county, or 0.8% claimed to know both Irish and English, and these were in the older age-groups. The other 99% claimed to know English only. Busy, marketing, midland towns like Mullingar or Athlone, the doorway to Connacht, were English-speaking long before the Famine. By 1861, not a single person in all of Westmeath spoke Irish only. Less than 500 (or 0.5%) of the total population of the county, claimed to know Irish. Other Leinster counties, like Offaly and Laois, Carlow and·Kildare, Wicklow and Wexford, had even smaller percentages. Kilkenny and Louth retained small pockets of Irish-speakers. By 1891, only 3½% of all of Leinster claimed any knowledge of the language. What is important to remember is that when people learned English, they did not become bilingual; they simply ceased to use Irish. Bilingualism was a middle-class luxury or dream of later and more prosperous times, which the struggling peasantry, small farmers and small shopkeepers in the nineteenth century could ill afford.

The anglicisation, which had already happened in Leinster and Ulster, was now also spreading throughout the Gaeltachts of Connacht and Munster. In 1871, the Census Commissioners noted, what they called, 'the rapidly progressing extinction of Irish as a spoken language'. Commenting on its disuse among the younger age-groups, they continued: 'thus it will be seen that spoken Irish is withering at the root and upwards all along the stem; within relatively a few years, Irish will have taken its place among the languages that have ceased to exist. . . fortunate, however. . . in the possession of a written literature which will embalm it for the study of the scholar, after it will have spent its final vibration upon the ear of man.'

With many in nineteenth century Ireland, Irish had become a matter of shame, It was a mark of inferiority to know Irish only, and it even became a matter of pride to some to be able to boast their ignorance of the Irish language. A generation of Irish people went through the saddening experience of being ignorant in both languages. A traveller in the country stated that everything about the people was 'patchwork' – their clothing, their dwellings, their language. Patchwork by choice can be artistic and colourful; patchwork by necessity is the outward mark of poverty and degradation. The Irish people had become the poverty-stricken victims of a patchwork culture. Scarcely able to read or write in either language, their Irish which was becoming increasingly poorer, was being replaced by a smattering of bad English. Because of the speed with which the language was being abandoned, and because parents with little English refused to communicate in Irish with their children, who had only poor English, a vast amount of traditional culture was lost. A generation of Irish people was being instilled with the lesson that cultural values should not be allowed to stand in the way of material progress. The language, and all that was associated with it, was seen to be cast away by one's parents and teachers and priests, as something that was not only worthless, but even damaging. The experience was bound to have detrimental psychological effects.

The people who were demanding and, let it be said,

acquiring the political and civil rights of nineteenth century England, and who were aspiring to the social, commercial and economic status of the English colonists in Ireland were only too eager to imitate their conquerors in the matter of language also, and adopted it as their own vehicle of communication, and as the measure of their advancement. It was seen as a victory of urban sophistication over rural backwardness, of 'townie' over 'culchie', of the richer farmlands over bog and mountainside, of the commercial economy of the eastern ports over the fishing villages of the west.

Douglas Hyde and other Gaelic Leaguers used to like to emphasise how the Gaelic League was radically different from every other language movement that had preceded it. This was in part the natural boast of men who were anxious to claim originality for their own movement. It is, indeed , true that the attempt to restore Irish as the spoken language of the country was a much more radical objective than the efforts of earlier societies to foster an interest in the ancient literature and history of the country. But one should not underestimate the significance of these earlier societies. Ever since the late eighteenth century individuals among the Anglo-Irish ascendency had displayed a romantic curiosity in the early literature and the material remains of Celtic Ireland. They encouraged the study of Ireland's distant past; and the collection, publication and preservation of its ancient learning, while there were still native scholars about to do the work.

Apart from the Royal Irish Academy, special organisations for the study of Ireland's ancient language and history were established throughout the nineteenth century. The Gaelic Society of Dublin was founded in 1806, followed by the Hiberno-Celtic Society in 1818; the Ulster Gaelic Society in 1830; the Irish Archaeological Society in 1840; the Celtic society in 1845; the Ossianic Society in 1853. All of these were associations producing material for scholars. They did not aim at converting the people over to a language policy.

Non-sectarian and non-political, these societies encouraged a progressive awareness of the value of the Irish language and literature. Among middle-class intellectuals they helped to restore some pride in a culture that was disappearing. A few individuals occasionally attempted to promote the spoken language among the people. But they could do very little to halt the tide of de-gaelicisation.

Among political leaders and propagandists, Thomas Davis alone advocated an Irish language revival policy. Influenced by what continental romantics were saying about their national languages, Davis asserted in *The Nation*, 'a people without a language of its own is only half a nation. A nation should guard its language more than its territories; 'tis a surer barrier and more important frontier than a fortress or river.'

The views expressed by Davis made little impact in their own time. They would not be taken up seriously until the end of the century. Official Fenian policies, concentrating on the establishment of the Irish Republic, had nothing to say about the language. Constitutional nationalism, from the days of O'Connell to Parnell simply ignored Irish. O'Connell's attitude was typical. As a native speaker he knew a great deal more Irish than did Thomas Davis. Yet he could witness without a sigh the gradual disuse of Irish because he regarded English as the more useful medium of modern communication.

In order for the Irish masses to become more politically conscious and to be educated into modern Irish Nationalism, they had first to take up English. This was the language of Grattan's Parliament, of the United Irishmen, of the ballads of '98, of Emmet's speech from the Dock, of Moore's patriotic songs, of *The Nation* newspaper. Through O'Connell, Young Ireland, the Fenians, the Land League and Home Rule, political nationalism was developed among the people in general and with little or no thought for the language that was being simultaneously abandoned. For the people had first to become nationalistic-minded through English before they could become aware of the political importance of a national language.

Meanwhile, in 1877, another association was established called the Society for the Preservation of the Irish Language. This was in many ways the ancestor of the Gaelic League. It was not so upper class in membership as were the earlier societies, and it reached out to the ordinary people by producing small cheap books of instruction in Irish, and texts for use in the Intermediate Schools. Unlike the earlier societies it concentrated on the cultivation and preservation of modern Irish. A patron of the society was Archbishop Croke, and one of its most active members was Michael Cusack, both of whom were shortly to be involved in the foundation of the Gaelic Athletic Association in 1884. The attempt to encourage the teaching of Irish in the schools was described by the London *Times* as 'predetermined futility'. The preservationists replied that preservation and the general replacement of English by Irish were two very different things, and that the replacement of one language by the other was neither possible nor desirable. It would only injure commerce and international trade and prevent Irishmen from participating in government and from occupying those positions which they had attained as a result of their own political power and intelligence. Only ten years later, on 31 July 1893, the Gaelic League was launched by men who had been associated with this society – Hyde, MacNeill and O'Neill Russell, precisely for the purpose of displacing English from the position it had come to hold on the tongues of the Irish people.

From what has already been said about the state of the language during the nineteenth century, its rapid rate of decline, the utilitarian attitude of the people towards it, and the powerful agencies of anglicisation at work in the country, it will be seen that the Gaelic League had set itself a monumental task. It called for tremendous love of the language, and faith and missionary dedication to the objects of the League on the part of its founders and organisers. Hyde, McNeill, O'Growney, Hickey and Pearse and their colleagues were well endowed with these virtues. To work as they did, they had to believe unreservedly in their own propaganda: that the Irish Nation was dead when the last Irish speaker was no more; that the native language was the best claim they had on the world's recognition of Ireland as a separate nation; that for as long as they spoke English they would remain poor imitations of the English people in everything else as well – literature, music, dress, games and ideas; that the soul of Ireland was to be rediscovered, not in the descendants of the colonists who sat in Grattan's Parliament, but in the Irish-speaking folk, the descendants of the hewers of wood and drawers of water.

Starting slowly enough, the Gaelic League had caught the imagination of the country by the early years of the twentieth century. Organisers travelled throughout the country establishing branches, which by 1904 had grown to just under 600. The League had its own weekly bilingual paper, *An Claidheamh Soluis*, and its own journal, *The Gaelic Journal*. O'Growney's *Simple Lessons in Irish* and the League's pamphlets and leaflets sold successfully. In one month alone, November 1906, it was calculated that the League sold over twelve and a half thousand copies of its publications. In the local branches instruction in the language was varied with classes in dancing, music and lectures on history and literature. Irish colleges were established in the Gaeltacht to give summer courses for language teachers. The activities of the League took on many of the best features of adult or community education and entertainment. At feiseanna throughout the country competitions were held and awards given for singing, dancing, spoken Irish and folktales. A whole new literature in modern Irish grew up under the mantle of the League. It set a trend in popular culture and was especially fashionable and influential among the educated lower-middle classes of the towns. It was less successful in the Gaeltacht. So while the real Irish-speaking districts continued to dwindle, more people in the anglicised east of the country could now claim to know Irish.

The extent of the League's success can be measured at one level by the Census returns. In 1891, that is, two years before the establishment of the League, in an anglicised county like Carlow, 123 persons, or 0.3% admitted to being able to speak Irish. Twenty years later, in 1911, 1008 persons, or 2.8% claimed to be able to speak it. Similar increases were recorded in every other Leinster county with the notable exception of Kilkenny (which had of course the largest number of genuine Irish-speakers in the province, but these were diminishing at a faster rate than the Gaelic League's Irish-speakers were increasing). In Connacht, and Munster generally, where there was native as distinct from Gaelic League Irish, the Census figures showed a continuing drop in the number of Irish-speakers. Overall then, the Gaelic League had established the trend which has continued down to the present, under native governments committed to revival policies. The number who claimed to be able to speak Irish was increasing, while at the same time, the decay in the Gaeltacht continued. Despite real achievement in spreading a love and knowledge of the language in the anglicised parts of the country, the League failed to preserve the language in the Gaeltacht. No doubt the language would have disappeared more rapidly without the activities of the League.

The linguistic revolution, therefore, had a partial success only, but the ordinary person's attitude to the language did change. If the man in the street, or in the field, did not share the enthusiasm of the Gaelic Leaguer for the revival, a certain pride in the language of his ancestors had been restored to him. The shame, the sense of inferiority that had once been attached to the speaking of Irish had been generally dispelled as a direct result of the activities of the League. And this raises the question of the non-linguistic consequences of the League.

Pearse, in his more political days towards the end of his career, used to say that men had not gone into the Gaelic League for the sake of 'is' and 'tá': they joined for the sake of Ireland. It is indeed true that the League attracted support from men like D. P. Moran of *The Leader*, who were more interested in publicising the philisophy of Irish-Ireland generally, than in advocating the learning of Irish. Encouraged by such men, the League had become more than a language movement. It became also a well organised, highly effective pressure group. It used its muscle to ensure that the teaching of Irish in the primary schools would be fully accepted, and it succeeded in having Irish-speaking children taught through their own language. In a famous battle before the Commission on Intermediate Education in 1899, the League successfully defended the inclusion of Irish in the Secondary School pro-gramme. Through a series of public meetings, deputations, pamphlets, a campaign in the press and the lobbying of support of the General Council of County Councils, who controlled the scholarship funds, the League put pressure on the new National University of Ireland to make Irish an essential subject for the Matriculation. Despite the very formidable opposition of University senators, including eminent churchmen like Archbishop Healy of Tuam, Dr Mannix, President of Maynooth and Dr Delany, President of the Jesuit University College on St Stephen's Green, the League had its way. This victory had the practical repercussion of making Irish essential in all secondary schools, where pupils might aspire to proceeding to the colleges of the National University.

It is arguable that too much of the League's energies were being diverted away from its own real work, towards the schools and colleges, the managers, teachers, curricula and examinations. But the pressure did not stop there. Public opinion was organised on a variety of social and economic issues that were regarded by the League as important for the nation. For example, it turned St Patrick's Day into a national holiday and closed the pubs on that day; it organised industrial parades and promoted 'Buy Irish' campaigns; the Post Office was forced to accept mail addressed in Irish; the courts were brought to recognise Irish as a legitimate language in which to advertise one's trade; and Dublin County Council agreed to favour for appointment to official posts candidates who had a knowledge of Irish. For a few years in the first decade of the twentieth century, whenever the League flexed its muscles, the country seemed to respond. It took on all the appearance of a giant killer. It had humbled the Senate of the National University. It challenged the bishops; it criticised Maynooth; it denounced Trinity and it talked down to the Irish Parliamentary Party.

By its own constitution, the Gaelic League was non-political, But it has to be said that it was non-political only in the strict and narrow party sense of that word. It officiallly avoided becoming involved in the political argument between the Home Rulers and the Unionists. But on any issue of nationality, it considered itself to have the right and the duty to speak for the nation. As Pearse said, even in his more intensive Gaelic League days: the League did not teach the doctrine of no politics; on the contrary, it taught Irishmen to take an intelligent interest in everything that bore on the national welfare. It was the duty of every Gaelic Leaguer, therefore, to concern himself with the political life of the nation.

Despite its protestation about being non-political, the Gaelic League had always been closely connected with Irish Nationalism. Its objectives were clearly those of cultural nationalism. Its origins and the warmth with which it was received by the people had been made possible only because of the intensity of Irish politics fostered by Parnell and the Land League. Its co-founders, Hyde and MacNeill, had also consciously followed the successful democratic models of the Land League and the Fenians.

The 1890s and the first half decade of the twentieth century were years of the Parnellite split and of Tory ascendancy. These years when there was something of a breathing space in the politics of Home Rule, corresponded with the halcyon days of the Gaelic League. The Gaelic League was at the height of its power when Arthur Griffith launched the Sinn Féin policy in 1905. The IRB was reorganised with the return of Tom Clarke in 1907, and a short time later it was revitalised with the accession of a number of activists into its ranks – the most talented of these were already in the Gaelic League. Sinn Féin, as well as the IRB, came under the strong influence of the League. With the Home Rule Bill of 1912, the political question took the centre of the stage once again, and the Gaelic League as an organisation went into decline. Its policies, however, were by now being promoted by every nationalist organisation and party in the country, and Gaelic Leaguers were taking their place in the van of the new nationalist movement. It was MacNeill who called for the establishment of the Irish Volunteers in 1913. When, in 1915, a majority of the executive committee of the League no longer even pretended to be non-political but changed the constitution to include in its objectives the independence of Ireland, Hyde, who had been President of the League since its foundation, resigned. Pearse, who had been editor of *An Claideamh Soluis* for years, inspired the 1916 Rising. And the first meeting of Dáil Éireann in January of 1919, was conducted largely in Irish. The League's political impact could hardly have been made any clearer.

Yet, the relationship between the League and the political movement for Independence was perhaps more subtle than direct. It had created the climate which was turned to good effect by the revolutionaries. Its cultural nationalism had provided the most intellectual arguments for their cause. And separatist, republican Ireland had its deepest justification in the philosophy of the League. If not quite the mother that Pearse had made it out to be, the Gaelic League had been at least the nurse to the political revolution. If the League had never been founded, conceivably there could have been a 1916 Rising, but it would have been one that would have lacked the cultural meaning given to it by men who were convinced that they had re-entered into their mystical birthright through the Gaelic League.

Before Independence, the Gaelic League had argued that Ireland was a separate nation because she had her own language. Nationalists drew the conclusion that because Ireland was a nation she had the right to independent statehood. After 1922, the New state took on official responsibility for the language revival, at a time when enthusiasm for the voluntary effort had waned or been deflected into politics. But an independent Irish state no longer had the need to prove the case for independence and so the argument of the language lost much of its political force. It was in this sense, then, that Pearse was right. With 1916, the appointed work of the Gaelic League was done.

12. Partition

Ronan Fanning

Partition, the division of our country, looms so large in our present that we too readily forget how recently it has become part of our past. Its origins, like the origins of so many other milestones in modern Irish politics, may be found in the Act of Union of 1800 which created the United Kingdom of Great Britain and Ireland. That act declared, among many other things, that the union so created was indissoluble, that the bonds then tied could never afterwards be broken. At first, and for three quarters of a century, that claim did not seem unduly extravagant at a time when the forces for union appeared almost irresistible. So rare, indeed, were British opponents of the union that the name of 'unionist' had yet to come into general usage. Nor did Irish opponents of the union appear to pose a dangerous threat. Revolutionary opposition – whether in the form of the followers of Emmet, or of the Young Irelanders in 1848 or of the Fenians in the 1860s – was spasmodic and impotent in the face of a mighty and complacent British empire and an increasingly self-confident Irish Catholic Church. The plight of those Irish constitutional opponents of the British connection who chose to work through the processes of parliamentary democracy was little better. The great majority of Irish members elected to sit in the Westminister parliament before 1874 simply aligned themselves in accordance with the existing framework of British party politics – Whig or Liberal on one side, Tory or Conservative on the other. The notable exception was Daniel O'Connell's repeal party in the twenty years after 1832 but even they never won as many as half of the Irish seats.

What changed things was the slow but inexorable advance of democracy. By the middle of the last century only some 165,000 Irishmen – and, as in the rest of the United Kingdom, no women – enjoyed the right to vote. The broadening of the franchise under the terms of the Electoral Reform Act of 1868 seemed miniscule: it increased the number of voters to 223,000 or just over 4 per cent of the total population. But even that small increase together with the introduction of secret voting following the ballot act of 1872 sufficed to give the new home rule party 60 of the 103 Irish seats – the first time a clear majority of Ireland's elected representatives formed a distinct and identifiably Irish nationalist party committed to the proposition that the union settlement must be altered. The decisive shift came only after another electoral reform act, in 1884, more than trebled the number of Irish voters to just short of three quarters of a million – more than 14 per cent of the population. Henceforth Irish elections were sufficiently democratic to ensure that the nationalist aspirations of the majority of the Irish people were effectively translated into a decisive majority of Irish parliamentary representation. The point was first plainly seen in the 1885 election returns when Parnell's party won 85 of the 103 Irish seats; and in all subsequent elections before 1918 the home rulers won a remarkably consistent 80 to 85 seats.

But the protagonists of Partition were the opponents, not the supporters, of Home Rule and it was the 1885 election which also revealed the peculiar geographic and demographic contours of Irish democracy which enabled them to lay claim to a democratic mandate within the north-eastern corner of the island. With the exception of the enclave of Dublin University, the nationalists won every seat in Ireland in 1885 outside the counties of Antrim, Armagh, Derry, Down and Tyrone. But in the bloc of the four north-eastern counties of Antrim, Armagh, Derry and Down, the nationalists won only 3 of the 18 seats – and not one of the 4 Belfast seats. The explanation for this electoral geography was, of course, a different demographic pattern first established as far back as the Ulster Plantation of the seventeenth century. Where the 1881 census had shown massive Catholic majorities in the other provinces Catholics were in a minority of 48 per cent in Ulster and in much smaller minorities in some counties – 23 per cent in Antrim and 31 per cent in Down.

These few statistics reveal why it was that 1885–86 witnessed the most significant shifts in Anglo-Irish relations since 1800. The first such shift was the dramatic announcement of

Gladstone's conversion to the cause of Irish Home Rule in December 1885. The second was the birth of Ulster Unionism as a distinct, coherent and powerful political force determined to resist Home Rule at whatever cost.

The impact of the commitment of Gladstone and his Liberal Party to Home Rule upon the landscape of Anglo-Irish relations was cataclysmic. It meant that the Union settlement of 1800, hitherto regarded as sacrosanct and indissoluble, was effectively declared to be negotiable. Still more significant was the fact that the Irish question became and – until the outbreak of the First World War in 1914 – remained the biggest single question dividing the British political parties. Previously the Union had been the principal test of political allegiance determining one's place in the Irish political spectrum; now the same was true of British politics.

This was because the Conservative Party became as quickly and firmly committed to defending the Union as Gladstone and the Liberals were to dismantling it. The Tories did this for two reasons: the first ideological, the second electoral. In so far as the Conservative Party had an ideology (and like most conservative parties they were scornful of ideology) it was the ideology of empire. To argue for the strength of imperial ties all over the world made little sense if Ireland, the country to which the British were geographically closest and with which they had the longest history of past association, were permitted to loosen their links with London at the very moment when Tories were arguing for the strengthening of imperial links elsewhere. 'Ireland,' declared the Conservative Prime Minister, Lord Salisbury, 'must be kept, like India, at all hazards; by persuasion, if possible; if not, by force'. The pragmatic argument was the simple one of electoral advantage. If Gladstone went for Home Rule, Lord Randolph Churchill early announced, then the Orange card would be the card to play; and, he added, 'I pray to God it proves the ace of trumps and not the two.'

The key to understanding the tenacity with which the Tories fought election after election in defence of the Union for the next 25 years was their conviction that the Orange card *had* proved the ace of trumps. Gladstone, unable to carry his party with him, saw it split asunder in 1886 when he could not carry

Home Rule even through the House of Commons. The Liberal party never fully recovered from that split. Those Liberals who seceded from the party set themselves up as an independent party, known as the Liberal Unionists, who gradually became almost indistinguishable from the Conservatives. One result of this alliance was to counteract the effect of Irish parliamentary party support for Gladstone. It ensured that for the next 20 years (with the exception of a short interlude between 1892 and 1895) only Conservative governments held office.

This is one explanation why the campaign for Home Rule proceeded at so snail-like a pace. Another explanation was the power which the House of Lords retained to veto any legislation initiated by the Commons. The Lords, a hereditary non-elective body where the Conservatives consequently possessed a permanent inbuilt majority, remained the biggest single obstacle in the path of Home Rule until their powers were reduced by the Parliament Act of 1911. They had shown their strength by throwing out Gladstone's second Home Rule Bill passed by the Commons in 1893. Indeed Conservative power in the Lords so inhibited the Liberals that when they finally achieved an overall majority (in the election of 1906) they made no attempt to re-introduce Home Rule until, following the elections of 1910, they were once more reduced to dependence upon Irish party votes for their parliamentary majority.

Partition attracted little attention in the twenty years after 1886 if only because no progress was then made towards resolving the Irish question. The attraction of Partition, in British eyes, was as a compromise – a compromise between satisfying what the Liberals saw as legitimate Irish national aspirations and what the Conservatives insisted were legitimate Unionist inhibitions. But before 1914, the dynamic of British politics made for confrontation not compromise on the Irish question.

The Tories, having between 1906 and 1910 suffered three electoral defeats in succession (an experience they have never subsequently had to endure) remained wedded to the notion that the Orange card was their last chance of electoral success. Hence the unprecedented extremism of Bonar Law's leadership of the Tory party after 1911 when he publicly declared that there were no lengths of resistance to which Ulster would go in which he would not be ready to support her. It was statements such as these which did nothing to discourage, if they did not positively provoke, such episodes as the Ulster gun-running of 1914 and the Curragh mutiny which pushed Britain to the brink of civil war. Tory extremism was in part designed to force the Liberals into holding yet another election on the Irish issue. That the Liberals refused to do so only confirmed the Tories in their view that they would win such an election.

The Unionists' campaign against Home Rule, led by Edward Carson after 1910, was opposed to partitionist compromises for other reasons. Carson, it must always be remembered, was a southern Unionist whose ultimate ambition was to use the vehemence and violence of Ulster Unionism to defeat Home Rule for Ireland as a whole. Privately, by the autumn of 1913, Carson was ready to concede that 'on the whole, things are shaping towards a desire to settle on the terms of leaving Ulster out', although he acknowledged the difficulty of defining Ulster. Publicly he contemptuously rejected Asquith's and Redmond's offer that any Ulster county might vote itself out of the Home Rule Bill for a limited period of six years.

However, as the 1912-14 crisis over Home Rule deepened, partitionist compromises were increasingly canvassed, both privately and publicly, within Asquith's government. Ministers like Lloyd George and Winston Churchill, in particular, were insistent on the necessity for making some sort of accommodation with the Ulster Unionists. But the Liberals remained dependent on Irish party support and the continuous pressure and promptings of John Redmond and his colleagues deterred them from openly embracing a partitionist solution before the outbreak of the First World War.

The coming of war changed everything. Since 1886 Ireland has been the football of British party politics, the most important single issue differentiating Liberals from Conservatives, the touchstone of party political faith. This was especially true in the months immediately preceding the outbreak of war when the struggle for the third Home Rule Bill was at its height and when civil war seemed imminent. But the Great War changed all that. Henceforth British political parties, united in pursuit of the supreme national interest of victory against Germany, were concerned with what bound them together, not with what forced them apart. The dynamic of party politics no longer made for confrontation but for consensus and, on the Irish issue, the search for consensus led British politicians inexorably down the partitionist path.

The full extent of the changes wrought in Anglo-Irish relations by the Great War only became explicit in May 1915 with the formation of the first coalition government. All the most notable of the Irish Parliamentary Party's adversaries during the bitter battles over Home Rule now became members of the government: Bonar Law, Austen Chamberlain, Walter Long, Arthur Balfour – men who had spent much of their political lives extending, in come cases, back to the 1880s, defending the Union – now obtained Cabinet appointments. So too, and this was the bitterest blow of all for the Irish at Westminister, did Edward Carson, the leader of the Ulster Unionists.

The importance of the fact that the Irish policy laid down in Whitehall and in Westminister from now until 1922 was the policy of a coalition goverment can scarcely be exaggerated. And it is here we discover a large part of the explanation for the emergence of partition as a compromise demanded by the interests of coalition government. Liberals and Conservatives were now allies, not enemies, and it was in neither side's interest that the embers of Irish controversy should be raked over any more than was absolutely necessary.

Two quite different consequences followed from this. First, both Liberals and Conservatives were disposed, as they had not previously been disposed, to avoid the Irish issue as much as possible for fear of the strains it might place upon the coalition partnership they both wished to uphold. Second, *if* the Irish nettle had to be grasped, there was an incentive towards a compromise solution, an agreed government policy, of a kind quite lacking in the normal workings of the British party political system as it had developed in the last quarter of the nineteenth century. The impetus, simply, was now towards agreement on Ireland where, previously, it had been towards disagreement. Agreement, in effect, meant taking into account the demands of the Ulster Unionists for special consideration; and that, in turn, meant some form of partition.

So much became clear during the Anglo-Irish negotiations which followed the 1916 Rising and which David Lloyd George conducted on behalf of the British government with John Redmond and with Edward Carson as the respective leaders of Irish nationalism and of Ulster Unionism. The negotiations broke down because Lloyd George negotiated separately with Carson and with Redmond who both came to a quite different understanding of his basic proposal. Carson understood that the government proposed to bring the Government of Ireland Act of 1914 into immediate operation while permanently excluding the six north-eastern counties from the terms of the act. Redmond understood that this exclusion would only be temporary. Once the anomaly became public knowledge, the negotations were doomed to failure.

Why was it that Redmond and Carson were more willing to contemplate in 1916 what they had rejected in 1914? The Rising and the execution of the revolutionary leaders that followed it was a more serious threat to Redmond's position than anything that had gone before. He desperately needed a settlement to bring home to Ireland to convince nationalist opinion that he could deliver the goods – to prove that the way of parliament was more effective than the way of revolution. Under these circumstances his resistance to some form of temporary partition became less obdurate: a Home Rule parliament which controlled twenty-six counties was better then no Home Rule parliament.

The partitionist aspect of Lloyd George's proposal, on the other hand, was precisely what attracted Carson and the Ulster Unionists. It was what they had sought and failed to obtain in the last round of Irish negotiations before the outbreak of the Great War. That Ulster would in the event receive separate and special treatment was, of course, highly probable; but the fact remains that, until 1916, the British government and parliament had continued to treat the Irish problem as a single problem, denying to Ulster that formal separateness she had so persistently demanded and was so shortly to attain.

Although Lloyd George's efforts in 1916 were short-lived and unsuccessful, they were nevertheless a clear pointer to the likely course of British policy. They provide the first concrete example of the stranglehold which the Unionist members of the coalition could exert upon the government's Irish policy from now until the coalition fell in 1922. In effect that stranglehold amounted to a power of veto. The power lay in the fact that for Unionists, unlike the other groupings attached to the coalition, there was an issue which ranked in importance with the conduct of the war: the issue of Irish policy. If their wishes were disregarded on Ireland they were ready to resign, as Carson did twice, even to put the government at hazard, whatever the state of the war. Their potential for this kind of blackmail was a most powerful weapon and one which greatly inhibited the coalition leaders, and in particular Lloyd George, from undertaking any initiatives in the area of Irish policy.

Nor is it insignificant that the 1916 negotiations represent Lloyd George's most radical and forceful attempt to solve the Irish problem for the duration of the war. In Irish policy as elsewhere Lloyd George showed scant respect for party precedent or programme. As early as 1910 he had tried to persuade the then leader of the Tory opposition, Arthur Balfour, to support a scheme he had drawn up for a Liberal-Conservative coalition, a national government with a national programme which included a vague scheme to solve the Irish problem along bi-partisan lines. An equally pragmatic approach underlay his attitude to the 1916 negotiations which were, he declared, the last chance of a settlement before the war was over.

Never again throughout the war or throughout the peace conferences which immediately followed did Lloyd George make another serious, personal effort to come to grips with the Irish problem. One reason why he was ready to attempt in the summer of 1916 what he did not again attempt until the autumn of 1919 was that he had not yet become Prime Minister.

He had much less to lose, therefore, from a single-handed

effort to solve the Irish problem. If he succeeded, it would be a fantastic feather in his cap. If he failed where so many had failed before him, it was unlikely to diminish his reputation. Once he became Prime Minister, however, as he did on 6 December 1916, he had neither the energy nor the inclination to take on the Irish problem. He had been appointed to that office as the man who would win the war and all his strengths were directed to that solitary objective. If he had learnt nothing else from his abortive Irish negotiations of 1916, moreover, he had learnt Ireland's unique potential for disruption and disunification within a coalition government: now he, as Prime Minister, had most to lose from such disruption.

Finally, the Lloyd George negotiations are important for Anglo-Irish relations insofar as they may be seen as a bridge, a kind of middle ground, between the negotiations of 1914 and the negotiations of 1920-21. The arguments and the issues are the same kind of arguments and issues with which we are familiar from 1914; in 1916, as in 1914, Redmond and Carson are the protagonists. Never again before the settlement of 1921-22 were representatives of the British government, of the Unionist majority in Ulster and of the nationalist majority in the rest of Ireland to come together to try to solve the Irish problem within a common framework of reference – a framework which derived its meaning from the fact that all three parties were participants in the United Kingdom parliament at Westminster. Even here, perhaps, one should ask whether Lloyd George's preference for negotiating separately with Carson and with Redmond might not be yet another illustration of the coalition's tendency to regard Ireland and Ulster as separate problems needing separate treatment.

The 1918 election, fought by Lloyd George's coalition *as a* coalition in the immediate and emotional aftermath of victory in war, further committed the British government to the partitionist path. Further Irish policy, declared Lloyd George, was governed by two facts: first, that the commitment to Home Rule (already on the statute book) must be honoured; second, that there should be no attempt 'to coerce an unwilling Ulster into accepting the rule of a Dublin parliament'. The first was designed to satisfy the Liberals, the second the

Conservatives and the combination finely calculated to hold the coalition together.

The consequences of that commitment did not become apparent until twelve months later when the special cabinet committee on the Irish question reported. The government's Irish policy, the report declared, was:

> limited in two directions. On the one hand the government was committed against any solution which would break up the unity of the empire. On the other, it was committed that Ulster must not be forced under the rule of an Irish parliament against its will. The first condition, therefore, excludes any proposal for allowing Ireland or any part of Ireland to establish an independent republic; the second precludes them from again attempting what has so often failed in the past, the establishment by the action of the Imperial Parliament of a single parliament for all Ireland on the line of the Home Rule Acts of 1886, 1893 and 1914.

The alternative course recommended by the committee and duly adopted by the government was to establish not one, but two parliaments in Ireland. It was embodied in the Government of Ireland Act passed in December 1920 and as a result of which Ireland remains partitioned until the present day.

The story of how the British government became committed to partition as their solution to the Irish problem is a complex one, here necessarily simplified. But enough, I hope, has been said to demonstrate a fundamental truth about Anglo-Irish relations too frequently ignored in Ireland. The Irish policy of British governments is not dictated by any objective concern for the harmony of Anglo-Irish relations but, at best, by subjective assessments of the British national interest; and, at worst, by short-term calculations of party political advantage. So it has always been. So it seems likely to remain.

13. The European Economic Community

John A. Murphy

On New Year's Eve 1972 there were the usual celebrations,
and on the stroke of midnight revellers at such places as
Christchurch in Dublin and Shandon Steeple in Cork, gave
expression to that mixture of nostalgia, hope and goodwill
which the human heart is conditioned to feel as the year turns.
This was no ordinary New Year, however. As the bells 'rang
in' 1973, the Republic of Ireland became a member of the
European Economic Community. Though there was little
evidence that the public revellers were acclaiming their new
destiny in Europe, there were many solemn, not to say
pretentious, pronouncements on the historic moment, and the
event was marked in various ways. On New Year's Day, an
insurance company announced the award of ten free policies
to newly-born 'European' babies – in Ireland, of course. A
famous firm of rose-growers produced a Euro-rose. School
children won essay prizes on the theme of Irish membership
of the EEC, a special European-marked silver piece was
presented to President de Valera, and nine trees were planted
on the canal bank to represent the nine members of the brave
new Europe. (Ireland, it appears, was represented by a willow
and the *Irish Times* sententiously noted a proverb: 'Willows
are weak, yet they bind other wood.') Yet despite this high
awareness in certain circles of a vital milestone in the nation's
history – a perception shared by anti-EEC groups who
regarded this New Year's Day as a time of mourning – the
public mood on the most momentous event since
independence was one of indifference.[1] In the years that
followed, the indifference turned into monumental boredom
– a paradoxical reaction to an institution that was daily
affecting the lives and living standards of the people. The
curious fatalism at the time of entry was in part a surfeited

response to an unduly protracted national debate, which had gone on intermittently during the 1960s.

The official interest in the Common Market – the usual description at the time – went back a long way to the eagerness to transcend the bonds of geographical insularity, post-war isolation and the confines of protectionism. The economic recovery of the late 1950s encouraged outward thinking. Membership of the Council of Europe and the OECD, and the conclusion of the Anglo-Irish Free Trade Agreement of 1966 had been steps along the way. The remarkably independent foreign policy stance of the early 1960s had been imperceptibly modified to take account of our prospective membership of the EEC, and our horizons swivelled around, as it were, from the United Nations to Western Europe.[2] The Irish application for membership was originally lodged on 31 July 1961 in Seán Lemass's time but it twice fell an incidental victim to General de Gaulle's veto of Britain. (From the beginning, therefore, our own application was a side-effect of Britain's.) When the Cross of Lorraine was lifted from the shoulders of France and her partners in 1969, it was time to begin again. The serious negotiations which got under way in June 1970 between Ireland and the Community culminated in the formal signing of the treaty of accession at the Egmont Palace in Brussels on 22 January 1972. There was to be a five-year transition period for phasing out industrial tariffs but Irish farmers would begin to benefit immediately from the EEC price support system, and farm export subsidies.[3] A constitutional amendment was necessary, because otherwise the new EEC arrangements would conflict with the emphasis in Bunreacht na hÉireann on independence and sovereignty,[4] and specifically with the provisions which asserted the exclusive rights of the Oireachtas and the Courts in the making and interpreting of laws.[5] The referendum would also, of course, be a plebiscite on entry. In the first half of 1972 the great debate became sustained and intense, and it filled the airwaves, the television screens, the newspaper columns and the ears and eyes, albeit already half-closed, of the plain people of Ireland.

The protagonists were far from evenly matched, since the pro-Marketeers, as we may call them, were superior in organisation, resources and political muscle. But there was a more equal division in terms of plausible arguments and debating skills, and media coverage was not ungenerous to the weaker side. The alignment of the pro-entry groups was curious in that the two main parties in the State, mutually antagonistic since their foundation, now campaigned on the same side. For one Fine Gael Euro-enthusiast, the persuasive and knowledgeable Garret FitzGerald, the advocation of membership was something of a crusade. Farming and business organisations also supported entry, and it particularly infuriated the anti-Marketeers that some State-sponsored bodies took a partizan stance, using public money to do so.[6] The anti-EEC groups were weak and fragmented and the intensity of their opposition varied considerably. The Labour Party, though far from unanimous on the issue, and the trade union movement, believed that the country's economy was insufficiently developed for Common Market competition. Other elements shared these misgivings but had their own political and ideological objections in addition. The divided wings of Sinn Féin, Official and Provisional, fought separate campaigns, and other anti-Market activists organised themselves in such small bodies as the Irish Sovereignty Movement and the misleadingly styled Common Market Defence Committee.

Opponents of entry compared the proposed membership with the Act of Union whose mythology had such powerfully adverse connotations for Irish nationalists – the sellout of independence for the fleshpots, effected by treachery, threats, bribes and frauds; the decay of the national economy and the eclipse of Irish industry because of massive, unfair competition; and, not least, the image of absentee politicians making whoopee in foreign capitals. Rather cleverly, the anti-Marketeers reminded their listeners that pro-Union advocates in *their* time had also promised a bright future, and Lord Clare was quoted to the effect that the superior wealth, skill and power of the stronger partner must necessarily benefit the weaker.[7] Against the invocation of such a powerful nationalist myth, there was no real historical counter-ploy except perhaps an attempt to use the millennial theme implicit in the most famous sayings of Parnell and Michael Collins. There was no boundary to the march of a nation and if freedom could be used to achieve more freedom, then it could be argued that membership of the EEC would enhance the nation's opportunities to realise its full potential.

The arguments most commonly put forward were about the likely effects of membership on prices, jobs and living standards, and it is probable that the final decision was arrived at on the basis of mundane self-interest, individual or national. Of course, the EEC proponents entered various caveats – we would have to work hard, there would be no begging bowl, Europe did not owe us a living, and so on. At the same time, they were driven by their own propaganda needs to exaggerate the benefits of membership. They depicted the future for Irish industry as bright: a Department of Foreign Affairs pamphlet said there would be 50,000 more jobs in industry by 1978 and predicted vast markets, with Ireland as an attractive location for new industry.[8] The really glittering prospects, however, were held out for agriculture: under the Common Agricultural Policy there would be high guaranteed prices and the endemic depression of Irish farming would be lifted. Mr Alan Dukes believed membership would give an 'opportunity to remodel the face of rural Ireland',[9] and Mr T. J. Maher, President of the IFA, said that 'the spectre of surpluses leading to the rapid decline in prices will be largely removed'.[10]

The anti-Marketeers on the other hand forecast soaring inflation and massive job losses. The meat processing industry would decline as the export of live cattle was stepped up.[11] The CAP, it was claimed, was only a temporary expedient and the EEC masterminds would implement a cheap food policy as soon as the Mansholt strategy had taken effect, driving the small farmers off the land.

Occasionally, the debate took on a loftier, if more nebulous tone. The great European statesmen of post-war reconstruction – Monet, Schumann, de Gasperi, Adenauer – were invoked to claim that the EEC was no mere customs union, no mere *zollverein* and that it had a nobler destiny. It would be a realisation of the European dream, a new Christendom. And Ireland, it was suggested, could contribute to this exciting grand design.[12] Had we not illuminated the darkness of Europe in the long ago through our saints and scholars? Could not we be 'the saviours of idealism' for Europe, in Patrick Pearse's phrase?[13] This was heady stuff, indeed, but it begged several questions, not least the galloping pace of secularism in the Ireland of 1972.

At this rarefied level of argument, there was no reply forthcoming from the anti-Marketeers, unless we count the ludicrous leaflet circulated to religious houses by the Common Market Defence Committee, sounding dire warnings about the threat to Ireland's faith and morals from the paganising forces which had already greatly weakened Christianity in Europe.[14]

Only slightly less unrealistic than the Christendom motif was the argument about how the Irish language and what was left of a distinctive culture would fare in the EEC. Would our cultural dependence on Anglo-American values be checked, and our own identity all the more cherished in the rich diversity of European culture or would our frail heritage be further swamped in a sea of European cosmopolitanism? At the end of 1972, Maolsheachlann O Caollaí, the anti-EEC secretary of the Gaelic League, pointed out that the Irish language would have no real status as a Community language, after all.[15]

There were examples on the two sides of trying to have the argument both ways. The anti-Marketeers claimed that with our clean air and open spaces we would be totally over-run by Europeans if we joined the EEC, and that we would be an exotic mecca for European tourists if we did not. On a much more serious level, the pro-Marketeers asserted – though the claims are not necessarily contradictory – that it was absolutely essential to join in order to achieve economic independence of Britain, and absolutely essential to join in order not to lose the vital British market. The latter point told heavily with the electorate who were never convinced by the anti-Marketeers that there was a real alternative to membership.

The EEC debate coincided with a dramatic peak in the Northern conflict in early 1972 and a surge of anti-British feeling in the South in the wake of Bloody Sunday in Derry. Not surprisingly, then, the question of the North loomed large in the arguments about entry. Here the advocates of membership made some very plausible points indeed. In the

EEC, tariff barriers between North and South would come down, economic and social differences would tend to diminish, cross-border projects under Community sponsorship would foster mutual goodwill, and Northern farmers would recognise that their interests lay with the South. As the Taoiseach, Jack Lynch, pointed out on the eve of the referendum poll,[16] if the Republic stayed out and the UK (including the North), as seemed inevitable, went in, the border would be further copperfastened. But, anyway, the seemingly intractable problem would surely become less so when transferred from the narrow ground to the enlarged Community, which would be bound to use its influence and its resources to deal with what would be, after entry, a domestic European problem. And, after all, if France and Germany could settle their historic animosities within the healing arms of the Community, surely the conflicting Irish traditions, recognising their common European identity, could be reconciled within the same therapeutic familial embrace. This kind of facile optimism characterised both the Fine Gael and the Fianna Fáil parties. Dr Garret FitzGerald in his *Towards a New Ireland* (London, 1972), pp. 104-05, blithely predicted that contact with foreigners would tend to accentuate a sense of common identity among all Irish people. And the same good cheer was exuded in a radio interview on New Year's Eve 1972 by the newly-appointed Minister for Foreign Affairs, the perennially ebullient Mr Brian Lenihan. Some pro-Marketeers invoked the potently palliative effects of the cup of tea or the glass of beer being sipped in common by Orange and Green in Brussels and Strasbourg. In the event, or at least in the short term, Community fora (such as the newly-elected European Assembly on opening day) turned out to be battlefields rather than chambers of peace for the conflicting Irish traditions. The optimistic predictions proved to be woefully wide of the mark, and even that most loyal servant of 'Europe', Commissioner Richard Burke, was moved to reflect ruefully in 1982 that the EEC had done little in the case of Northern Ireland to effect the reconciliation which was what the Community was all about in the first instance.[17]

Of the non-economic issues, however, sovereignty loomed

larger than unity, and the argument here had to do as much with national psychology as with the legal and political position. Sovereignty would be gravely impaired in the EEC, the anti-Marketeers claimed, we would no longer have the power to keep Irish land in Irish hands, and we would be under pressure by our new partners, all of whom belonged to NATO, to abandon our neutrality.[18] Above all, it would be a shameful betrayal of our history if the State relinquished some of that sovereignty so hardly won and so briefly enjoyed. Was not that, indeed, so the story went, the very objection to entry which President de Valera, that great champion of sovereignty, was privately expressing? In Cork, Seán Hendrick, steely intellectual, veteran of the Civil War, great friend and contemporary of Frank O'Connor and Seán Ó Faoláin, had campaigned against membership on the fundamental issue of sovereignty. In the year or so before his death in October 1971 he had preached the gospel in private company and at public meetings and he maintained that to join the EEC was to violate Article 9.2 of the Constitution which enjoins 'fidelity to the nation and loyalty to the State' as 'fundamental political duties of all citizens'.

The advocates of entry briskly countered the 'sovereignty' argument by asserting that the concept was an illusion in an inter-dependent world, particularly so for a weak and isolated state on the periphery of Europe. No nation-state in isolation could plan its trade or control the environment or protect commonly shared values. Nominal sovereignty, as the Taoiseach pointed out on the eve of the poll,[19] could frequently cloak a real dependence on external forces. Voluntary participation with our partners in discussions about matters affecting us could increase our power to influence decisions, and thus in real terms strengthen our sovereignty. Yes, replied the anti-Marketeers, but *our* input into the discussions would be negligible and the interests of the big states would still be dominant.

As for neutrality, said the pro-Marketeers, the Treaty of Rome was not concerned with such matters and we could continue to keep out of military pacts. On the other hand, as Sean Lemass had long since made clear, we were never neutral ideologically and would not be found wanting when it came to defending western values. Yes, a common foreign and defence policy was one day envisaged as the Community moved towards real union, but that was in the far-off future and the Irish people would be consulted again as new issues arose. In the pro-Marketeer argument about neutrality, it should be said, there was a vein of ambiguity which has continued to characterise the subject to this day.

After a last frantic bout of campaigning, the referendum was held on 10 May 1972. Considering the widely-publicised historic nature of the decision about to be made, the turnout of 71.09% of the electorate was hardly dramatic. The anti-Marketeers had never really expected to win, but neither they nor their opponents anticipated the dimensions of the landslide. 1,041,890 voted for the amendment validating entry while there were only 211,891 against. It was 83.1% to 16.9%, almost five to one. No previous turning-point had been so massively endorsed by the people – not Sinn Féin's victory in 1918, nor the Anglo-Irish Treaty in the election of 1922, nor yet the Constitution of 1937. However, 'in a land where to fail is more than to triumph', to quote Stephen Gwynn, the 17% continued to take a morose pride in their stand, and in the subsequent decade of growing popular disenchantment with the EEC (as the surveys were to show), people boasted of belonging to the 17% in 1972, in much the same way as countless Volunteer veterans were reputed to claim a presence in the GPO in 1916.

For the moment, however, the result was devastatingly beyond dispute.. The Irish Sovereignty Movement predicted grave threats to the very fabric of Irish society and, later on, Tomás Mac Giolla of Official Sinn Féin stated that entry meant the destruction of the 1916 proclamation, especially 'the right of the people of Ireland to the ownership of Ireland and to the unfettered control of Irish destinies.'[20] The victors were jubilant. David Andrews of Fianna Fáil believed the result indicated that reunification was getting nearer. 'This is one of the great and triumphant moments of our history', said George Colley of the same party, and then in a patriotic purple sentence he added 'tonight the indomitable are truly on the way back from Kinsale'.[21] It was also noted by commentators that, in Northern Ireland where there was no referendum, the result could hardly have been welcome to unionists – that is, to the extent that they were interested at all. Curiously, unionists and republican socialists were alike opposed to the EEC, the former because they smelt a Dublin-Romish conspiracy as well as fearing adverse effects on the North's economy from UK membership, the latter because they saw the Community as part of the strategy of international capitalism.

In all the tumult of the debate, little attention had been given to the far-reaching second sentence of the constitutional amendment, now so overwhelmingly endorsed. What it said was this: 'No provision of this constitution invalidates laws enacted, acts done or measures adopted by the State necessitated by the obligations of membership of the Communities or prevents laws enacted, acts done or measures adopted by the Communities, or institutions thereof, from having the force of law in the State' (Art. 29.4.3°). Whatever the constitutional lawyers might say, it sounded to the lay person very much like a *carte blanche* clause, subordinating the whole Constitution to the diktats of the European Commission at Brussels. It could hardly have pleased Eamon de Valera to sign the relevant legislative measures providing for what some extremists described as the subversion of Bunreacht na hÉireann.

When the time came for formal accession, at the New Year in 1973, the sense of historic change was widely voiced by, among others, newspaper editors, captains of industry and ecclesiastical leaders. 'Our most important decision since independence', was how the 1972 *Irish Times Annual Review* described it. The Catholic bishops waxed eloquent about Ireland's place in Europe, and solemnly declared that 'our national life at every level – religious, cultural, intellectual and social – will be profoundly affected by the step we are about to take'. Their lordships referred sentimentally to our fellow-Europeans as 'old friends', 'gratefully remembering' our past contributions and ready to welcome us back.[22] This affecting picture was at odds with the record. The historical evidence points either to European indifference to this country over the centuries, or to the cynical exploitation by Europeans of Ireland for their own strategic purposes. Irish Jacobites, for example, were conscious that they were being *used* rather than *helped* by Louis XIV. When the Young Irelanders were given the brush-off by the leaders of the second French Republic (who were anxious to stay on the right side of the British), John Mitchel drew a Sinn Féin moral for his own and future generations: 'We must thank M. Lamartine for teaching us that in the end we must rely on ourselves'.

After the euphoria *and* the gloom of entry, membership began to take its effect at various levels. There were, however, two further developments in 1979 which were also hailed by EEC supporters as epoch-making. One was the Republic's participation in the European Monetary System, with its promise of stability in the exchange rate. In the event, the move failed to halt inflation; it created an ailing native currency; and the historic step of breaking the link with sterling, it could be argued, added both a fiscal and a psychological dimension to the problem of partition. The other much-heralded 'European' event was the holding of direct elections to the European Assembly on 7 June 1979. Despite lavish funding, the elections created very little excitement, North or South. Since the Assembly lacked the characteristics of a real parliament, most of the electorate refused to take it seriously, and regarded the scramble for seats as the pursuit of well-paid jobs for the boys and girls. Some of the successful Irish candidates enjoyed the fleshpots of Strasbourg for a time, but soon realised that the real political action was still at home. Overall, the Assembly tended to be regarded as a piece of window-dressing, an attempt to put a representative democratic face on a bureaucratic institution. Nor was it clear that the Irish members – or at least, the Fianna Fáil party – were eager to see the Assembly's powers extended, since this would diminish still further the prerogatives of the Oireachtas.[23] Besides, who knew? An Assembly with real teeth might impose post-Christian values on Holy Ireland.

In the years after entry, the Community idea was widely and constantly publicised in Ireland. To be critical of membership was to be regarded as irresponsible and eccentric. There was no shortage of expensively-produced information brochures on the Community. Adult education courses were saturated with EEC propaganda, and subsidised trips to

Brussels, Strasbourg and Luxembourg were the order of the day. The writer admits to having been a beneficiary – but only once – of such a joyride to Strasbourg. Politicians, civil servants, judges, EEC legal experts, academics and business people developed new career dimensions. One's perception of Ireland's role in the EEC frequently depended on whether one was getting a piece of the action. Irish diplomats and government ministers tried to be 'good Europeans' in a way inexplicable to their British, or in another sense, their French colleagues. Outside the charmed circles mentioned, Irish people 'felt' no more nor no less European than they had done before membership. Our sense of identity, and the dwindling fortunes of the Irish language, were not affected one way or the other. Strangely, the hoped-for dramatic expansion in the learning of European languages did not take place, and Irish business people continued to be at a disadvantage in this respect.

But membership impinged soon enough on Irish lives in all kinds of areas. In the nature of things, the drawbacks were perceived rather than the advantages. Irish people were reluctant to accept that Europeans were now on the same footing as themselves in matters that ranged from fees for higher education to the setting up of businesses, and this realisation vaguely rankled, as did the imposition of directives from the Commission on matters great and small. Of course, there were considerable net benefits in cash and development projects, and our export trade was certainly diversified but there was disillusionment over astronomical price increases, a pathetic regional policy, a grave decline in manufacturing industry, and mounting unemployment. Ten years after entry, there were 15,000 fewer employed in manufacturing industry.[24] Some of these unfortunate developments, it could be argued, stemmed from the energy crisis and the world recession. Still, there was substance in the point that membership and the Brussels orientation in themselves had sapped the *national* will to tackle *national* problems. The begging bowl mentality had, if anything, been aggravated.

Membership also seemed to mean endless wrangles about quotas and limits and prices in fisheries and agriculture. A strange way to conduct the business of the new visionary

Europe, people might be forgiven for thinking. The row about fisheries was particularly bitter since a long-neglected native resource had only recently been begun to be developed and now, so it seemed, it had to contend with the ruthlessly efficient fishing practices of our new partners. The fishing controversy was only one example of the conflict between the old economic nationalism and the new European imperatives. The 'Buy Irish' campaigns, whose roots were deep in Irish nationalist history, were seemingly inconsistent with the spirit of the Community, if not the letter of its law, especially if supported by Irish government funds. After all, the concept of 'foreign' no longer applied to our Community partners, and the Irish purchaser was suppose to regard Italian shoes with the same patriotic affection as Cork or Dundalk footwear.

Though Ireland still retained her military neutrality ten years after entry, the neutralists saw danger in the growth of the European Political Co-operation idea and the increasing tendency of the member States to harmonise their foreign policies.[25] What significant input, your confirmed neutralist might ask, had Ireland into policies effectively determined by former imperial powers, with extensive strategic and economic interests abroad? Had Ireland ever attempted to press disarmament policies on her partners? How long more would Ireland, as the only non-NATO member of the Community, be allowed to make fine distinctions between the political and military aspects of security? What had we to say to the officially EEC-commissioned Tindemans report of 1976 which stressed the need for a common defence policy? Rather than reply to these knotty questions, the Irish 'Europeans' could point to positive advantages in an anomalous situation. Ireland, they could claim, had a real voice in world affairs through the EEC. And our unique non-military role meant that the Community did not have the image of a NATO subsidiary, while African and Latin-American countries saw Ireland as moderating the European political process, and humanising its economic policy towards developing nations.

The legal ramifications of membership were extensive and complex.[26] The EEC law-making machinery added continually to domestic law. Several thousand directives and regulations, welcome and otherwise, poured out from the Community since 1973 and were implemented here. Complaints about the bureaucratic and undemocratic nature of such law-making have to be measured against the real achievements of EEC-inspired reform – in company law, for example. The most far-reaching changes are still in progress in the field of women's rights in employment opportunities and equal pay, stemming ultimately from what might be called the Women's Charter article, Article 119 of the Treaty of Rome which stresses 'the application of the principle that men and women should receive equal pay for equal work'.

The great attraction of membership in the beginning had been the guaranteed high prices for farm produce and increased living standards for farmers. Despite a serious slump in 1974, there had been several years of remarkable farming prosperity, though the rural economy was never really reconstructed as the optimists had hoped. The Common Agricultural Policy came under increasing fire from the larger countries which favoured a cheap food policy. Finally, in the first half of 1983 the enormous expense of running the Community was linked with the intolerable burden of maintaining the CAP, and a milk super levy was threatened in an attempt to cut back production, and reduce the cost of subsidies. If implemented, this would undo all the gains derived by Irish farmers from membership. Farming spokesmen described it as the greatest crisis since entry and as a grave threat to the living standards of the whole people. There were complaints that the rules of the EEC game were being changed against our will, and in some circles the unthinkable opinion was beginning to be voiced that we should 'pull out', if necessary.[27]

However, a number of crucial questions remained to be asked when this collective *ologón*-ing had subsided. Was the CAP ever really a defensible policy? Whom had it benefitted other than the big farmers? Was the money from it in the good years used to acquire land rather than for productive investment and development? Where had all the CAP windfall gone? Of the £3 billion benefits of membership, £2.5 billion had come through the Farm Fund.[28] Most important question of all – if the CAP no longer fitted, should we continue to wear the rest of the Community clothes?

Whatever the answers, a decade is too short a period in history on which to decide the really momentous question: has Ireland's membership of the EEC been a millstone or a milestone, a wrong turning or a great leap forward?

Notes

7. The Act of Union

Further Reading

The outstanding secondary source on the Union is G. C. Bolton, *The Passing of the Irish Act of Union. A Study in Parliamentary Politics,* Oxford 1966. This can be supplemented by R. B. McDowell, *Irish Public Opinion 1750-1800,* London 1944. Still invaluable is W. E. H. Lecky, *A History of Ireland in the Eighteenth Century,* 5 vols, London 1892, especially vol. V. A useful collection of primary material with introductory notes has been published by the Public Record Office of Northern Ireland as Education Facsimiles 41-60, *The Act of Union.* Contemporary pamphlets are an invaluable source for public opinion and the attitudes and machinations of the politicians can be studied in their printed correspondence, e.g. W. Beresford, ed., *Correspondence of the Rt Hon. John Beresford,* 2 vols, 1854, Marquess of Londonderry, ed., *Memoires and Correspondence of Viscount Castlereagh,* 4 vols, 1848-54, C. Ross, ed., *Correspondence of Charles, first marquis of Cornwallis,* 3 vols, 1859. Extracts from William Pitt's correspondence are to be found in Ashbourne, *Pitt: some chapters of his life and times,* 1898 and A. P. P. Roseberry, *Pitt.* 1892.

1. James Carty, *A Junior History of Ireland.* London 1948 ed., p. 57.
2. J. G. Swift MacNeill, *The Constitutional and Parliamentary History of Ireland till the Union.* Dublin and London 1917, pp. 381-2.
3. Useful treatments of the Irish parliament and the electorate are to be found in E. M. Johnston, *Great Britain and Ireland 1760-1800.* Edinburgh 1963, parts II and III. See also J. L. McCracken, *The Irish Parliament in the Eighteenth Century.* Dundalk 1971.
4. *The Speeches of the Right Hon. Henry Grattan.* Dublin, no date, p. 70.
5. Bolton, *Act of Union,* pp 53-4.
6. *Ibid.,* p. 12.
7. H. Senior, *Orangeism in Ireland and Britain, 1795-1836.* London 1966, p. 4. This view is now open to question; see W. H. Crawford, 'Change in Ulster in the late eighteenth century' in T. Bartlett and D. W. Hayton, *Penal Era and Golden Age.* Belfast 1979, p. 203.
8. Bolton, *Act of Union,* p. 54.
9. *Ibid.,* p. 46.
10. *Ibid.,* p. 157.
11. P.R.O.N.I., *The Act of Union.* Education Facsimiles, 41-60, no. 50.
12. Bolton, *Act of Union,* pp. 216-22.
13. *Ibid.,* chapter V.
14. Carty, *Junior History,* pp. 58-9.
15. Louis Cullen, *An Economic History of Ireland since 1660.* London 1972,

pp. 98–105; Joseph Lee, 'Grattan's Parliament', in Brian Farrell, ed., *Irish Parliamentary Tradition*. Dublin 1973.

16. A. P. W. Malcomson, *John Foster. The Politics of the Anglo-Irish Ascendancy*. Oxford 1978, p. 432.
17. Malcomson, *John Foster*, p. 77.

13. The European Economic Community

1. For the above, see *Irish Times*, 30 December 1972, 1 and 2 January 1973.
2. Patrick Keatinge, *A Place among the Nations* (Institute of Public Administration, Dublin, 1978), esp. pp. 161, 165–168, 209–221.
3. Calendar of events leading to entry, *Irish Times*, 1 January 1973, p. 13.
4. Arts. 1 and 5.
5. E.g. Art. 15.2.1°.
6. *Irish Times*, 10 May 1972. See pro-EEC advertisements by An Bord Bainne and The Pigs and Bacon Commission in the daily newspapers, 9 May 1972.
7. *Irish Times*, 1 January 1973, reporting an address by Mícheál Ó Loingsigh to the Irish Sovereignty Movement on 30 December 1972. The meeting, it was noted, was attended by only 100 people.
8. *Into Europe: Ireland and the EEC* (Department of Foreign Affairs, Dublin, n.d.), p. 4. See also *Opportunity: Ireland and Europe* (Irish Council of the European Movement, Dublin, 1972), for the principal pro-entry arguments.
9. *Irish Times Annual Review*, 30 December 1972.
10. *Irish Times,* 1 January 1973.
11. E.g. as in 7 above.
12. Cf. bishops' statement, *Irish Times*, 29 December 1972.
13. Quoted by David Thornley, 'Patrick Pearse', *Leaders and Men of the Easter Rising*, ed. F. X. Martin (Dublin, 1911), pp. 155–56.
14. *Irish Times*, 10 May 1972.
15. *Irish Times*, 1 January 1973.
16. *Irish Times*, 10 May 1972.
17. *Ireland in Europe 1973-83* (Dublin Office of the Commission, December 1982), p. 5.
18. The anomaly of non-NATO Ireland's membership of the EEC was evident from the beginning: see Dennis Kennedy's article in *Irish Times Annual Review*, 30 December 1972.
19. *Irish Times*, 10 May 1972.
20. *Irish Times*, 1 January 1973.
21. *Irish Times*, 12 May 1972.
22. *Irish Times*, 29 December 1972.
23. Point made by Jack Lynch, *Irish Times*, 7 June 1979.
24. See article by Seamus Brennan, *Sunday Tribune*, 31 July 1983.
25. See paper entitled 'Ireland and EPC' by Padraic MacKernan, Assistant Secretary and Political Director, Department of Foreign Affairs, read to Royal Irish Academy, National Council for the Study of International Affairs, 4th Annual Conference, 20 November 1981. Two articles by

Dennis Kennedy in the *Irish Times* on 10 and 11 May 1983 discuss the ambiguity in the concept of Irish neutrality in the EEC context. See also the controversy (reports in Irish newspapers, 14 January 1983) that followed the European Assembly's endorsement of a report urging closer co-operation between EEC and NATO.

26. For an expert survey of this area, see Bryan M. E. McMahon, 'EEC membership and the Irish legal system', *Ireland and the European Community*, ed. P.J. Drudy and Dermot McAleese (Cambridge University Press, 1984).

27. For the initial stage of the superlevy crisis, see daily and Sunday papers in late July 1983.

28. See Colm Boland, 'European Diary'. *Irish Times*, 23 July 1983; Paul Tansey, 'The CAP just does not fit', *Sunday Tribune,* 1 April 1984.

The Great O'Neill

Seán O'Faolain

The Great O'Neill first appeared in 1942 and the intervening years have only confirmed the book's standing as a modern classic and Seán O'Faolain's stature as one of the most distinguished of living Irish writers.

For nine years O'Neill resisted English expansion, became one of the most famous soldiers in Europe, wore out Elizabeth I, broke generals like Essex and Brough, involved Spain and Rome. Through these pages pass papal legates, government spies, great monarchs, statesmen, cutthroats, poisoners, passionate women, traitors and brave men. But, for all its drama, this book remains a work of scholarship and is likely to stand as the authoritative story of a crucial period of Irish history.

'May be commended to the historian for its breadth and freshness of view and the brilliance of its writing.'

The Times Literary Supplement

'A series of pictures of wild grandeur and outlandish brilliance set against a background of Renaissance colour and turmoil.'

Sunday Times

'A vivid fascinating picture of Elizabethan Ireland.' *Irish Times*

Leaders and Workers

Edited by J. W. Boyle

Here are portraits of nine men (William Thompson, John Doherty, Feargus O'Connor, Bronterre O'Brien, James Fintan Lalor, Michael Davitt, William Walker, James Connolly, James Larkin) whose lives between them span a century and a half, linking the days of the United Irishmen with our own. They include a forerunner of Marx, Chartists, trade union pioneers, champions of tenant farmers' and women's rights, leaders in the Irish and British labour movements. Though they came from different backgrounds, each of them, whether reformer or revolutionary, thinker or socialist – and some filled most of these roles – desired, like Thomas Russell, to alter conditions in which property was put before life. Even the least successful gave their followers in bleak and bitter times a fresh sense of human dignity and informed them with some of their own passion for the creation of a society freed from inequality and injustice. It is this passion that makes the lives and ideas of these nine Irishmen of continuing interest today.

Contributors: Patrick Lynch, Andrew Boyd, Asa Briggs, Thomás P. O'Neill, T. W. Moody, J. W. Boyle, Desmond Ryan, James Plunket

Michael Collins and the Treaty
His Differences with de Valera

T. Ryle Dwyer

To Michael Collins the signing of the Treaty between Ireland and Britain in 1921 was a 'Stepping Stone'. Eamon de Valera called it 'Treason'.

The controversy surrounding this Treaty is probably the most important single factor in the history of this country, not only because it led to the Civil War of 1922-1923 but also because the basic differences between the country's two main political parties stem from the dispute.

T. Ryle Dwyer not only takes an in-depth look at the characters and motivations of the two main Irish protagonists but also gives many insights into the views and ideas of the other people involved on both sides of the Irish Sea.

This book is not only the story of Michael Collins' role in the events surrounding the Treaty, but it is also the story of his differences| with Eamon de Valera which were to have tragic consequences for the nation.

De Valera's Darkest Hour, 1919-1932
T. Ryle Dwyer

De Valera's Darkest Hour is the story of Eamon de Valera's struggle for national independence during the most controversial period of his career. It deals with his election as Priomh Aire of Dáil Éireann, his unauthorised assumption of the title of President, his controversial tour of the United States, his obscure part in the negotiations leading to the Anglo-Irish Treaty and his reasons for rejecting the Treaty. De Valera's misunderstood rôle in the period leading up to and during the Civil War, and finally his spectacular recovery in lifting himself from the despised depths of 1923 to become President of the Executive Council of the Irish Free State in less than nine years are covered in detail.

De Valera's Finest Hour, 1932-1959
T. Ryle Dwyer

Throughout his long career de Valera was a controversial figure but his greatest critics give him credit for his courageous denunciation of international aggression during the 1930s and for his adroit diplomatic skill in keeping Ireland out of the Second World War in the face of Nazi provocation and intense Allied pressure. His policy was guided by one paramount consideration – his concept of the best interests of the Irish people. He pursued those interests with such determination that he became the virtual personification of Irish independence.

Dr Dwyer gives a graphic account of de Valera's quest for independence. Of particular interest are well-chosen and carefully documented extracts from contemporary letters, speeches, newspaper articles, etc., giving many new insights into the thoughts and motives of this enigmatic politician, who has left an indelible imprint on Irish history.

The Years of the Great Test, 1926-1939
Edited by Francis MacManus

Twelve well-known writers give separate accounts of the years 1926-1939 in Ireland – a period just after the Irish Free State had been established and showing how men new to government dealt with problems that affected not only Ireland but the world.

The authors deal with social life, education, politics, literature, external associations, north-south relations. They survey the many aspects of life in the new Ireland with a real depth of understanding that should make an immediate appeal to those who are now benefiting from the seeds then sown.

'In the practical business of surviving, in developing new communities abroad, in assisting the sick and poor, also in avoiding extreme disparities in social relationships, that generation did not do too badly. It was certainly a good deal less spoilt than the present one.'
T. Desmond Williams

Contributors: T. Barrington, Vincent Grogan, David Kennedy, F. S. L. Lyons, Francis MacManus, Nicholas Mansergh, J. L. McCracken, James Meenan, Donal Nevin, Kevin B. Nowlan, Seán Ó Catháin SJ, David Thornley, Terence de Vere, T. Desmond Williams.

The Course of Irish History

Edited by T. W. Moody and F. X. Martin

Though many specialist books on Irish history have appeared in the past fifty years, there have been few general works broadly narrating and interpreting the course of Irish history as a whole, in the light of new research. That is what this book, first published in 1967, set out to do; and it is a measure of its success that it is still in demand, being now in its sixteenth printing.

The first of its kind in its field, the book provides a rapid short survey, with a geographical introduction, of the whole course of Ireland's history. Based on the series of television programmes first transmitted by Radio Telefís Éireann from January to June 1966, it is designed to be both popular and authoritative, concise but comprehensive, highly selective but balanced and fair-minded, critical but constructive and sympathetic. A distinctive feature is its wealth of illustrations.

The present edition is a revised and enlarged version of the original book. A new chapter has been added, bringing the narrative to the end of 1982, and the illustrations have been correspondingly augmented. The list of books for further reading has been expanded into a comprehensive bibliography of modern writings on Irish history. The chronology has been rewritten, updated, and much enlarged, so that it now amounts to a substantial supplement to the text. Finally, the index has been revised and extended both to include the new chapter and to fill gaps in the original coverage.

The book has been planned and edited by the late Dr T. W. Moody, fellow emeritus and formerly professor of modern history, Trinity College, Dublin, and Dr F. X. Martin O.S.A., professor of medieval history, University College, Dublin – an appropriate partnership for this enterprise of scholarly cooperation. Of the other 19 contributors, 17 are or were on the staffs of the universities and university colleges of Ireland and two were on those of the universities of Cambridge and of Manchester.